D0831296

cook's choice.
TASTY TREATS

Over 100 mouth-watering recipes

igloobooks

igloobooks

Published in 2013
by Igloo Books Ltd
Cottage Farm
Sywell
NN6 0BJ
www.igloobooks.com

OCE001 0813
4 6 8 10 9 7 5 3
ISBN: 978-0-85780-988-9

Food photography and recipe development: Stockfood, The Food Image Agency
Front and back cover images © Stockfood, The Food Image Agency

Printed and manufactured in China.

CONTENTS.

INTRODUCTION.

Wow! A whole book dedicated to the wonderful new sweet treat – whoopie pies. This book covers a huge selection of these yummy cakes, in all shapes, sizes, colours and textures, as well as other indulgent goodies including cookies, biscuits and tarts. And once you've mastered the whoopie pie, why not try macaroons?

So what is a whoopie pie? For those who haven't yet sampled the delicious, cream-filled sponges, a whoopie pie is a new craze that originated in America as a simple chocolate cake 'sandwich' and has grown into a worldwide phenomena with endless combinations. They come in every shape, size, shade and favour you can imagine sandwiched together with a sweet, creamy filling. Whoopie pies are also known as 'gobs', 'bobs', 'black-and-whites' or a 'BFO', which stands for 'Big Fat Oreo'!

The first section, dedicated to whoopie wonders, takes you through just a selection of the possible combinations of whoopie pies. Beginning with a basic recipe to get you started, moving on to simple pies, such as mini vanillas, chocolate cream and gingersnap whoopie pies. If you want to be more adventurous, there are plenty of ideas to choose from: you can experiment with food dye, creating red velvet pies, or alternatively fill them with fruit, cream, nuts, or anything else you can get your hands on, as well as decorating them with frosting, icing sugar, sprinkles, fruit, and so on… the possibilities are endless.

After nearly 100 pages of whoopie pie recipes, there are 2 whole chapters dedicated to other sweet treats to tempt your taste buds. There are cookies and biscuits that are perfect for any occasion. If you want to take the difficulty level a step further, there are recipes for filled biscuits, such as the cream-filled chocolate biscuits, lemon cream biscuits and lime curd shortbreads, as well as highly decorative chocolate hazelnut meringues, orange stars and heart-shaped jam biscuits. Indulge in decadent florentines, lavender biscuits and cranberry shortbread stars. There are even fun recipes for kids, like chocolate bean cookies and star-shaped biscuits.

Once you've mastered whoopie pies and conquered cookies, why not move on to macaroons, the classic dainty French dessert that inspired the whoopie pie movement. From classic macaroons, such as the Luxembergli and vanilla macaroons through to chocolate, fig, amaretti and pistachio. There is even an easy step-by-step guide at the beginning of the chapter, to show you all of the techniques for success.

HERE ARE SOME HINTS AND TIPS:

Use fresh, organic ingredients where possible, but don't worry if those products aren't available, the results will still be delicious!

Unless otherwise specified, your ingredients should all be at room temperature when you start. Butter should be soft, but not melted and where possible try to use unsalted butter.

Take your time to carefully read the recipes and ensure you have everything you need ready and prepared.

Make sure you have a mixing bowl big enough for all of your ingredients with enough room for mixing them without spillage.

Always sift dry ingredients, such as flour and icing sugar. It removes lumps and aerates the powder. This makes it easier to mix and produces a lighter texture.

Use caster (superfine) sugar where a recipe does not specify and remember that light brown, dark drown and muscavado are all different.

Electric whisks are great for whisking egg whites and creaming together butter and sugar. They speed up the mixing process, but are by no means necessary.

Hand whisks and spoons are perfectly good for mixing ingredients and come in handy if you need to smooth any lumps, or fold ingredients in gently.

Get your oven preheated, usually before you start mixing the ingredients, so that when you put your mixture into the oven it is at an even temperature.

The wide range of exciting recipes that follow are well-tested and are fully selected to ensure that they will suit both beginners and experts alike, so you can create spectacular desserts for all sorts of occasions.

WHOOPIE PIES.

Basic whoopie pies

Prep and cook time: 25 minutes * makes: 16

INGREDIENTS:

110 g | 4 oz | ½ cup butter
110 g | 4 oz | ½ cup caster
(superfine) sugar
2 eggs
1 tsp vanilla extract
225 g | 8 oz | 2 cups self-raising flour
½ tsp salt

METHOD:

Heat the oven to 180°C (160° fan) 350F, gas 4. Line 3 large baking trays with greaseproof paper.

Beat the butter and sugar in a mixing bowl until light and fluffy. Gradually beat in the eggs and vanilla until blended. Sift in the flour and salt and gently stir in until smooth.

Drop tablespoonfuls of the mixture onto the baking trays, evenly spaced, and spread them out a little to 7 ½ cm / 3 " diameter rounds.

Bake the whoopie pies for about 15 minutes, until cooked through. Insert a toothpick, if it comes out clean, they are done. Cool them on the baking trays for a few minutes, then place on a wire rack to cool completely.

Mini vanilla whoopie pies

Prep and cook time: 35 minutes * makes: 30

INGREDIENTS:

350 g | 12 oz | 3 cups plain
(all-purpose) flour
½ tsp baking powder
a pinch of salt
110 g | 4 oz | ½ cup butter
225 g | 8 oz | 1 cup sugar
1 large egg
225 ml | 8 fl. oz | 1 cup milk
2 vanilla pods (bean)

For the filling:
110 g | 4 oz | ½ cup unsalted butter
170 g | 6 oz | 1 ⅔ cups icing
(confectioners') sugar
½ tsp vanilla extract
450 g | 1 lb marshmallow cream

METHOD:

Heat the oven to 190°C (170° fan) 375F, gas 5. Line 3 large baking trays with greaseproof paper.

Sift the flour, baking powder and salt together then set the bowl aside. Beat the butter and sugar in a mixing bowl until light and fluffy. Gradually beat in the egg until blended.

Stir in the flour mixture and gently stir in until incorporated. Split the vanilla pods and scrape the seeds into the mixture. Stir in the milk and mix well.

Drop generous teaspoons of the mixture onto the baking trays, keeping them evenly spaced.

Bake for 5-7 minutes, until springy to the touch. Cool the sponge halves on the baking trays for a few minutes, then place them on a wire rack to cool completely.

For the filling, beat the butter and icing sugar with an electric whisk until blended. Continue whisking until fluffy, then add the vanilla and marshmallow cream and whisk until smooth.

Sandwich two sponge halves together with the cream filling and gently press together.

Chocolate cream cheese whoopie pies

Prep and cook time: 35 minutes * makes: 12-15

INGREDIENTS:

50 g | 2 oz | ⅓ cup chopped dark (plain) chocolate
175 g | 6 oz | ¾ cup butter
225 g | 8 oz | 1 cup sugar
2 eggs
1 tsp vanilla extract
250 g | 9 oz | 2 ¼ cups plain (all-purpose) flour
25 g | 1 oz | ¼ cup cocoa powder
2 tsp baking powder
¼ tsp bicarbonate of soda (baking soda)
½ tsp salt
120 ml | 4 fl. oz | ½ cup buttermilk

For the filling and topping:
110 g | 4 oz | ½ cup unsalted butter
400 g | 14 oz | 2 cups cream cheese
450 g | 16 oz | 4 ½ cups icing (confectioners') sugar
1 tsp vanilla extract
sugar sprinkles and stars

METHOD:

Heat the oven to 190°C (170° fan) 375F, gas 5. Line 3 large baking trays with greaseproof paper.

Melt the chocolate in a heatproof bowl over a pan of simmering water then set it aside to cool. Beat the butter and sugar in a mixing bowl until light and fluffy. Gradually beat in the eggs, vanilla and melted chocolate until blended.

Sift in the dry ingredients and gently stir in, then add the buttermilk, until smooth.

Drop tablespoons of the mixture onto the baking trays, about 7 ½ cm / 3 " in diameter.

Bake for 10-15 minutes, until firm to the touch. Cool on the baking trays for a few minutes, then place on a wire rack to cool completely.

For the filling and topping, whisk all the ingredients together with an electric whisk until smooth.

Spread the flat side of a cooled sponge with the filling. Place another half, flat side down, on top and then press together lightly. Place a spoonful of the filling on top of each whoopie pie and decorate with sugar sprinkles.

Chocolate whoopie pies with vanilla cream

Prep and cook time: 40 minutes * makes: 8

INGREDIENTS:

110 g | 4 oz | ½ cup butter
200 g | 7 oz | 1 cup light brown sugar
1 large egg
50 g | 2 oz | ½ cup cocoa powder
350 g | 12 oz | 3 cups plain
(all-purpose) flour
1 ½ tsp bicarbonate of soda
(baking soda)
½ tsp salt
1 tsp vanilla extract
250 ml | 9 fl. oz | 1 cup plain yoghurt
175 g | 6 oz | 1 cup chopped dark
(plain) chocolate

For the filling:
150 g | 5 oz | ¾ cup unsalted butter
250 g | 9 oz | 2 ½ cups icing
(confectioners') sugar
few drops vanilla extract

METHOD:

Heat the oven to 180°C (160° fan) 350F, gas 4 and line 3 large baking trays with greaseproof paper.

Beat the butter and sugar in a mixing bowl until light and fluffy and gradually beat in the egg.

Sift in the cocoa, flour, bicarbonate of soda and salt and gently stir in to combine, then stir in the vanilla and yoghurt.

Drop tablespoons of the mixture onto the baking trays and sprinkle the chopped chocolate on top.

Bake for 12-15 minutes, until cooked through and firm to the touch. Cool on the baking trays for a few minutes, then place them on a wire rack to cool completely.

For the filling, beat the butter until soft and creamy. Sift in the icing sugar and add the vanilla and beat well until smooth.

Spread the flat side of a cooled sponge half with the filling. Place another half, flat side down, on top of the filling then press both halves together lightly.

Raspberry whoopie pies

Prep and cook time: 30 minutes * serves: 8

INGREDIENTS:

110 g | 4 oz | ½ cup butter
110 g | 4 oz | ½ cup caster
(superfine) sugar
2 eggs
225 g | 8 oz | 2 cups self-raising flour
a pinch of salt
1 tsp raspberry liqueur
120 ml | 4 fl. oz | ½ cup milk
pink food dye (optional)

For the filling:

300 g | 11 oz | 1 cup raspberries
2 tbsp icing (confectioners') sugar
300 ml | 11 fl oz | 1 ⅓ cups cream

METHOD:

Heat the oven to 180°C (160° fan) 350F gas 4. Line 3 large baking trays with greaseproof paper.

Beat the butter and sugar in a mixing bowl until light and fluffy. Gradually beat in the eggs until blended. Sift in the flour and salt and gently stir in. Stir in the raspberry liqueur, milk and a few drops of food dye, if using.

Drop large, evenly spaced, tablespoons of the mixture onto the baking trays.

Bake for about 15 minutes, until cooked through. Cool the sponges on the baking trays for a few minutes, then place on a wire rack to cool completely.

For the filling, purée the raspberries in a blender, or crush them with a fork. Pass the purée through a sieve and stir in the icing sugar. Whisk the cream until stiff and fold it into the purée.

Sandwich two sponge halves together, flat side down, with the filling and gently press.

Gingersnap whoopie pies

Prep and cook time: 35 minute * makes: 6

INGREDIENTS:

110 g | 4 oz | ½ cup light brown sugar
100 ml | 3 ½ fl. oz golden (corn) syrup
110 g | 4 oz | ½ cup butter
110 g | 4 oz | 1 cup plain
(all-purpose) flour
3 tsp ground ginger
60 g | 2 oz | ½ cup unsalted
peanuts, chopped
60 g | 2 oz oats

For the filling:
4 egg whites
30 g | 1 oz icing (confectioners') sugar
200 ml | 7 fl. oz | ⅞ cup cream
4 tsp stem ginger syrup,
from a jar of stem ginger
1-2 tsp ground cinnamon

METHOD:

Heat the oven to 180°C (160° fan) 350F, gas 4. Line 2 large baking trays with greaseproof paper.

Heat the brown sugar, golden syrup and butter in a pan over a low heat, stirring continuously. When the sugar has dissolved, remove the pan from the heat and add the flour and ground ginger and stir well to combine.

Drop large tablespoons of mixture on the baking trays and scatter over the peanuts and oats.

Bake for 8-10 minutes, until golden brown. Leave to cool and become crisp.

For the filling, whisk the egg whites with an electric whisk until softly peaking. Add the icing sugar and continue to whisk until the mixture is stiff and glossy.

Whisk the cream until thick and gently fold it into the egg white mixture. Fold in the stem ginger syrup and cinnamon.

Spread the filling generously over half of the sponges and place the remaining sponges on top.

Maple walnut whoopie pies

Prep and cook time: 35 minutes * makes: 10

INGREDIENTS:

225 g | 8 oz | 2 cups plain
(all-purpose) flour
½ tsp salt
½ tsp baking powder
110 g | 4 oz | ½ cup unsalted butter
175 g | 6 oz | ¾ cup light brown sugar
75 ml | 2 ½ fl. oz | ⅓ cup maple syrup
2 large eggs
75 g | 2 ½ oz | ¾ cup walnuts,
finely chopped

For the filling:
225 g | 8 oz | 1 cup unsalted butter
250 g | 9 oz | 2 ½ cups icing
(confectioners') sugar
30 g | 1 oz light brown sugar
30 ml | 1 fl. oz maple syrup
50 g | 2 oz | ½ cup chopped walnuts

METHOD:

Sift the flour, salt and baking powder together and set aside.
Beat the butter, brown sugar and maple syrup together in a mixing
bowl until soft and creamy. Gradually beat in the eggs until blended.

Stir in the dry ingredients and walnuts until combined.

Heat the oven to 180°C (160° fan) 350F, gas 4. Line 3 large
baking trays with greaseproof paper. Drop a tablespoon
of the mixture at a time onto the baking trays.

Bake the whoopies for 9-12 minutes, until springy to the touch.
Cool on the baking trays for a few minutes, then place on a
wire rack to cool completely.

For the filling, beat the butter until soft and creamy. Sift in the
icing sugar and beat with an electric whisk until smooth.

Beat in the brown sugar and maple syrup and beat well until
blended. Stir in the walnuts.

Spread the flat side of a cold cake with a generous amount of filling.
Place another half, flat side down, on top of the filling and gently
press them together.

Strawberry marshmallow whoopie pies

Prep and cook time: 35 minutes * makes: 8

INGREDIENTS:

250 g | 9 oz | 2 ¼ cups plain
(all-purpose) flour
1 tsp bicarbonate of soda
(baking soda)
a pinch of salt
1 egg
80 ml | 3 fl. oz | ⅓ cup sunflower oil
225 g | 8 oz | 1 cup sugar
1 tsp strawberry extract
½ tsp pink food dye
150 ml | 5 fl. oz | ⅔ cup buttermilk

For the filling and topping:
225 g | 8 oz | 1 cup unsalted butter
200 g | 7 oz | 2 cups icing
(confectioners') sugar
200 g | 7 oz marshmallow cream
1 tsp vanilla extract

To decorate:
pink sugar sprinkles

METHOD:

Heat the oven to 180°C (160° fan) 350F, gas 4. Line 3 large baking trays with greaseproof paper.

Stir the flour, bicarbonate of soda and salt together. Whisk the egg, oil, and sugar together in a mixing bowl. Whisk in the strawberry extract and food dye. Gently fold in the flour mixture and add the buttermilk, until the mixture is smooth.

Drop tablespoons of the mixture onto the baking trays.
Bake for 10-15 minutes, until cooked through. Insert a toothpick, if it comes out clean, they are done. Cool on the baking trays for a few minutes, then place on a wire rack to cool completely.

For the filling and topping, beat the butter in a bowl until soft and creamy. Whisk in the remaining ingredients until the mixture is thick and smooth. Spread the flat side of a cooled sponge half with a generous amount of filling. Place another half, flat side down, on top of the filling then press gently.

Spread the remaining mixture on top of the whoopie pies and scatter with sugar sprinkles.

Mini chocolate whoopie pies

Prep and cook time: 30 minutes * makes: 20

INGREDIENTS:

110 g | 4 oz | ½ cup butter
110 g | 4 oz | ½ cup caster
(superfine) sugar
2 eggs
60 g | 2 oz cocoa powder
225 g | 8 oz | 2 cups self-raising flour
½ tsp salt
1 tsp vanilla extract
120 ml | 4 fl. oz | ½ cup milk

For the filling:
300 ml | 11 fl. oz | 1 ⅓ cups cream
1-2 tbsp icing (confectioners') sugar

METHOD:

Heat the oven to 180°C (160° fan) 350F, gas 4 and line 3 large baking trays with greaseproof paper.

Beat the butter and sugar in a mixing bowl until light and fluffy. Gradually beat in the eggs until blended.

Sift in the cocoa, flour and salt and gently stir, then add the vanilla and milk.

Drop teaspoonfuls of the mixture onto the baking trays in 2 ½ cm / 1 " diameter rounds.

Bake for about 12-15 minutes, until cooked through and firm to the touch. Cool on the baking trays for a few minutes, then place them on a wire rack to cool completely.

For the filling, whisk the cream until it is thick. Sift in enough icing sugar to taste. Spread the flat side of a cold cake with a some of the cream filling. Place another half, flat side down, on top of the filling then press both halves together lightly.

Whoopie pies with sugar candies

Prep and cook time: 40 minutes * makes: 10

INGREDIENTS:

125 g | 4 ½ oz | ½ cup butter
200 g | 7 oz | 1 cup caster (superfine) sugar
1 large egg
400 g | 14 oz | 3 ½ cups plain (all-purpose) flour
1 tsp bicarbonate of soda (baking soda)
½ tsp salt
225 ml | 8 fl. oz | 1 cup plain yoghurt
1 tsp vanilla essence

For the filling:
225 g | 8 oz | 2 ¼ cups icing (confectioners') sugar
100 g | 3 ½ oz | ½ cup unsalted butter
75 ml | 2 ½ fl. oz dulce de leche
1 vanilla pod (bean)

For the icing:
175 g | 6 oz | 1 ¾ cups icing sugar
1-2 tbsp water

To decorate:
sugar hearts and flowers

METHOD:

Heat the oven to 180°C (160° fan) 350F, gas 4. Line 3 large baking trays with greaseproof paper.

Beat the butter and sugar in a mixing bowl until light and fluffy. Gradually beat in the egg until smooth.

Sift in the flour, bicarbonate of soda and salt and gently stir in. Add the yoghurt until smooth and thick.

Drop tablespoons of the mixture onto the baking trays, about 4 cm / 2 " apart.

Bake for 10-15 minutes, until cooked through. Cool on the baking trays for a few minutes, then place on a wire rack to cool completely.

For the filling, beat the butter and icing sugar with an electric whisk until smooth. Whisk in the dulce de leche.

Split the vanilla pod and scrape the seeds into the mixture. Spoon it into a piping bag.

Pipe mixture onto the flat side of a cold cake and place another half, flat side down, on top of the filling, then press both halves together lightly.

For the icing, sift the icing sugar into a bowl and stir in just enough warm water to make a smooth, thick icing.

Spread the flat side of a cooled sponge with the filling. Place another half, flat side down, on top of the filling then press both halves together.

To decorate, sift the icing sugar into a bowl and gradually beat in enough water to give a smooth, thick icing. Spread the icing over the top of the whoopie pies. Decorate with sugar hearts and flowers.

Classic chocolate whoopie pies

Prep and cook time: 35 minutes * makes: 8

INGREDIENTS:

200 g | 7 oz | 1 ¾ cups plain (all-purpose) flour
a pinch of salt
½ tsp baking powder
½ tsp bicarbonate of soda (baking soda)
45 g | 1 ½ oz | ½ cup cocoa powder
110 ml | 4 fl. oz hot milk
175 g | 6 oz | ¾ cup light brown sugar
75 ml | 2 ½ fl. oz | ⅓ cup sunflower oil
1 egg
1 tsp vanilla extract
55 ml | 2 fl. oz buttermilk

For the filling:
400 ml | 14 fl. oz | 1 ⅔ cups cream
1 tsp vanilla extract
2-3 tbsp icing (confectioners') sugar

METHOD:

Heat the oven to 180°C (160° fan) 350F, gas 4 and line 3 large baking trays with greaseproof paper.

Sift the flour, salt, baking powder and bicarbonate of soda together.

In a separate bowl, mix the cocoa and hot milk together until completely dissolved,

Stir the sugar and oil until smooth and then whisk into the cocoa mixture until it is blended.

Whisk the egg, vanilla and buttermilk into the cocoa mixture until smooth.

Gently fold the dry ingredients into the cocoa mixture, until blended.

Drop tablespoons of the mixture onto the baking trays, making sure there is enough room for them to spread while baking.

Bake the pies for 10-15 minutes, until cooked through. Insert a toothpick, if it comes out clean, they are done. Cool them on the baking trays for a few minutes, then place on a wire rack to cool completely.

For the filling, whisk the cream and vanilla together until thick. Whisk in the icing sugar to taste. Spoon the cream into a piping bag.

Pipe the cream on the flat side of a cooled cake. Place another cake, flat side down, on top of the filling and gently press them together.

Whoopie pies with caramel cream

Prep and cook time: 45 minutes ∗ makes: 20

INGREDIENTS:

110 g | 4 oz | ½ cup butter
180 g | 6 oz | ¾ cup caster (superfine) sugar
2 eggs, beaten
350 g | 12 oz | 3 cups plain (all-purpose) flour
1 tsp baking powder
1 tsp vanilla extract
250 ml | 9 fl. oz | 1 cup buttermilk

For the filling:
300 ml | 11 fl oz | 1 ⅓ cups cream

For the caramel cream:
110 g | 4 oz | ½ cup sugar
30 ml | 1 fl. oz water
40 ml | 1 ½ fl. oz cream
2 egg whites
a pinch of salt
110 g | 4 oz | ½ cup butter, diced
½ tsp vanilla extract

METHOD:

Heat the oven to 180°C (160° fan) 350F, gas 4 and line 3 large baking trays with greaseproof paper. Beat the butter and sugar in a mixing bowl until light and fluffy. Gradually beat in the eggs until smooth.

Sift in the flour and baking powder and gently stir. Add the vanilla and buttermilk and blend well. Drop tablespoonfuls of the mixture onto the baking trays, keeping them about 4 cm / 2 " apart.

Bake the whoopie pies for about 15 minutes, until golden and cooked through. Cool on the baking trays for a few minutes, then place on a wire rack to cool completely. For the filling, whisk the cream until stiff and chill until ready to use.

For the caramel cream, gently heat half of the sugar and the water in a pan without stirring. When the mixture becomes deep amber, remove the pan from the heat, add the cream and stir until smooth.

Put the egg whites, salt, and the remaining sugar in a heatproof bowl over a pan of simmering water. Whisk the sugar until it dissolves and the mixture becomes hot. Remove the bowl from the heat.

Once the egg whites have cooled slightly, whisk to form stiff peaks. Whisk in the butter and continue whisking until smooth.

Whisk in the vanilla, followed by the warm caramel. Whisk for 4-5 minutes until smooth.

Place the caramel cream on half of the pies, and cream on the other half, sandwiching them together and press down gently.

Dark chocolate whoopie pies with white chocolate cream

Prep and cook time: 1 hour 30 minutes * makes: 12

INGREDIENTS:

125 g | 4 ½ oz | ½ cup butter
150 g | 5 oz | ¾ cup dark (plain)
chocolate, chopped
225 g | 8 oz | 1 cup sugar
3 eggs
1 tsp vanilla extract
250 g | 9 oz | 2 ¼ cups plain
(all-purpose) flour
30 g | 1 oz | ¼ cup cocoa powder
½ tsp baking powder

For the filling:
300 ml | 11 fl. oz | 1 ⅓ cups cream
75 g | 2 ½ oz white chocolate
vanilla extract

METHOD:

For the filling, heat the cream to boiling point. Remove from the heat and add the chocolate, stirring until melted. Stir in a few drops of vanilla and chill for at least 1 hour.

Heat the oven to 160°C (140° fan) 325F, gas 3 and line 3 large baking trays with greaseproof paper.

Melt the butter and chocolate in a heatproof bowl over a pan of simmering water.

Whisk the sugar, eggs and vanilla together in a mixing bowl, then gently fold in the chocolate mixture.

Sift in the flour, cocoa and baking powder and gently stir into the chocolate mixture. Place tablespoonfuls of the mixture onto the baking trays and bake for 8-10 minutes until firm to the touch. Cool on the baking trays for a few minutes, then place on a wire rack to cool completely.

Spread the flat side of a cooled sponge with a generous amount of filling. Place another half, flat side down, on top of the filling then press both halves together.

Victoria sponge whoopie pies

Prep and cook time: 35 minutes * makes: 8

INGREDIENTS:

110 g | 4 oz | ½ cup butter
110 g | 4 oz | ½ cup caster
(superfine) sugar
2 eggs
225 g | 8 oz | 2 cups self-raising flour
a pinch of salt
1 tsp vanilla extract
120 ml | 4 fl. oz | ½ cup milk

For the filling:
300 ml | 11 fl. oz | 1 ⅓ cups cream
300 g | 11 oz | 1 cup raspberry
jam (jelly)

To decorate:
24 raspberries
icing (confectioners') sugar

METHOD:

Heat the oven to 180°C (160° fan) 350F, gas 4 and line 3 large baking trays with greaseproof paper.

Beat the butter and sugar in a mixing bowl until light and fluffy. Gradually beat in the eggs until combined.

Sift in the flour and salt and gently stir in. Add the vanilla and milk. Drop tablespoons of the mixture onto the baking trays, about 4 cm / 2 " apart.

Bake for about 15 minutes, until golden and cooked through. Insert a toothpick, if it comes out clean, they are done. Cool the sponge halves on the baking trays for a few minutes, then place on a wire rack to cool completely.

For the filling, whisk the cream until stiff. Spread raspberry jam and put a spoonful of cream onto half of the sponges. Place the remaining halves, flat side down, on top then press both halves together lightly.

Place a few raspberries on top of each whoopie pie and sift a little icing sugar over the top.

Cranberry whoopie pies

Prep and cook time: 1 hour 20 minutes * makes: 10-12

INGREDIENTS:

125 g | 4 ½ oz | ½ cup unsalted butter
200 g | 7 oz | 1 cup caster
(superfine) sugar
1 egg, beaten
400 g | 14 oz | 3 ½ cups plain
(all-purpose) flour
1 ¼ tsp bicarbonate of soda
(baking soda)
½ tsp salt
270 ml | 10 fl. oz | 1 ⅛ cups buttermilk
½ tsp vanilla extract
110 g | 4 oz | 1 cup cranberries

For the filling:
225 ml | 8 fl. oz | 1 cup cranberry juice
150 g | 5 oz | ¾ cup
marshmallow cream
110 g | 4 oz | ½ cup unsalted butter
200 g | 7 oz | 2 cups icing
(confectioners') sugar

METHOD:

Heat the oven to 160°C (140° fan) 325F, gas 3 and line 3 large
baking trays with greaseproof paper.

Beat the butter and sugar in a mixing bowl until light and fluffy,
then gradually beat in the egg.

Sift in the flour, bicarbonate of soda and salt and gently stir in
alternately with the buttermilk, until combined. Stir in the vanilla
and cranberries.

Drop tablespoons of the mixture onto the baking trays about
4 cm / 2 " apart.

Bake for 10-15 minutes, until cooked through. Insert a toothpick,
if it comes out clean, the whoopie pies are done. Cool them on the
baking trays for a few minutes, then place on a wire rack to
cool completely.

For the filling, put the cranberry juice into a pan and increase the
heat to boiling point. Let the cranberry juice boil for 5-10 minutes
until it has reduced.

Beat the marshmallow cream and butter with an electric whisk
until smooth and fluffy.

Sift the icing sugar into the butter mixture and add the cooled
cranberry syrup, stirring to create a smooth cream.

Sandwich two halves together using a tablespoonful of the filling
and gently press them together.

Buttermilk whoopie pies

Prep and cook time: 40 minutes * makes: 12

INGREDIENTS:

125 g | 4 ½ oz | ½ cup butter
200 g | 7 oz | 1 cup caster
(superfine) sugar
1 large egg, beaten
400 g | 14 oz | 3 ½ cups plain
(all-purpose) flour
1 tsp bicarbonate of soda
(baking soda)
½ tsp salt
250 ml | 9 fl. oz | 1 cup buttermilk

For the filling:
175 g | 6 oz | ¾ cup unsalted butter
350 g | 12 oz | 3 ¼ cups icing
(confectioners') sugar
few drops vanilla extract

For the icing:
175 g | 6 oz | 1 ¾ cups icing sugar
1-2 tbsp water

METHOD:

Heat the oven to 180°C (160° fan) 350F, gas 4 and line 3 large baking trays with greaseproof paper.

Beat the butter and sugar in a mixing bowl until light and fluffy. Gradually beat in the egg until blended.

Sift in the flour, bicarbonate of soda and salt and gently stir in. Slowly add the buttermilk until smooth and thick, you may not need all of the buttermilk.

Drop tablespoons of the mixture onto the baking trays. Bake them for 10-15 minutes, until cooked through. Cool the sponge halves on the baking trays for a few minutes, then place on a wire rack to cool completely.

For the filling, beat the butter and icing sugar in a bowl until soft. Stir in the vanilla and beat until smooth.

Spread the flat side of a cooled sponge with a generous amount of filling, place another sponge half on top and press together gently.

To decorate, sift the icing sugar into a bowl and gradually beat in enough water to give a smooth, thick icing. Drizzle the icing over the top of the whoopie pies.

Red velvet cream whoopie pies

Prep and cook time: 40 minutes * makes: 12

INGREDIENTS:

225 g | 8 oz | 2 cups plain
(all-purpose) flour
75 g | 2 ½ oz | ¾ cup cocoa powder
1 tsp baking powder
¼ tsp bicarbonate of soda (baking soda)
¼ tsp salt
175 g | 6 oz | ¾ cup unsalted butter
150 g | 5 oz | ¾ cup sugar
1 large egg
1 tsp vanilla extract
1 tsp red food dye
60 ml | 2 fl. oz | ¼ cup buttermilk
120 ml | 4 fl. oz | ½ cup warm water

For the filling:
50 g | 2 oz | ¼ cup solid vegetable fat
50 g | 2 oz | ¼ cup unsalted butter
110 g | 4 oz | 1 cup icing sugar
1 tsp vanilla extract
120 ml | 4 fl. oz | ½ cup golden syrup

To decorate:
150 g | 5 oz | 1 ½ cups icing sugar
water, red food dye

METHOD:

Heat the oven to 190°C (170° fan) 375F, gas 5. Line 3 large baking trays with greaseproof paper.

Sift the flour, cocoa powder, baking powder, bicarbonate of soda and salt together. Beat the butter and sugar in a mixing bowl until light and fluffy. Gradually beat in the egg, vanilla and red dye until blended. In a separate bowl, mix the buttermilk and warm water together.

Gradually stir the dry ingredients into the butter mixture, then add with the buttermilk mixture until smooth. Drop tablespoonfuls of the mixture onto the baking trays. Bake for 8-10 minutes, until springy to the touch. Cool on the baking trays for a few minutes, then place on a wire rack to cool completely.

For the filling, beat the vegetable fat and butter with an electric whisk until soft and creamy. Gradually beat in the icing sugar and continue whisking until light and fluffy. Slowly whisk in the vanilla and golden syrup until the cream is light and smooth.

Spread half of the cooled sponges with the cream. Place another half, flat side down, on top of the filling then press both halves together lightly.

To decorate, sift the icing sugar into a bowl and add just enough water to form a smooth, thick icing. Add a few drops of red food dye and stir until smooth. Drizzle the icing over the top of each whoopie pie and leave to set.

Choc-chip peanut butter whoopie pies

Prep and cook time: 25 minutes * makes: 10

INGREDIENTS:

350 g | 12 oz | 3 cups self-raising flour
2 tsp bicarbonate of soda
(baking soda)
175 g | 6 oz | ¾ cup light brown sugar
a pinch of salt
1 egg
75 ml | 2 ½ fl. oz | ⅓ cup sunflower oil
150 ml | 5 fl. oz | ⅔ cup buttermilk
75 ml | 2 ½ fl. oz | ⅓ cup boiling water
75 g | 2 ½ oz | ½ cup chocolate chips
75 g | 2 ½ oz | ½ cup unsalted peanuts,
chopped

For the filling:
340 g | 12 oz jar peanut butter, unsalted

METHOD:

Heat the oven to 180°C (160° fan) 350F gas 4. Line 3 large baking trays with greaseproof paper.

Mix the flour, bicarbonate of soda, sugar and salt together in a mixing bowl.

Whisk the egg, oil and buttermilk together and mix them into the dry ingredients with the boiling water until smooth. Stir in the chocolate chips and peanuts.

Drop tablespoons of the mixture onto the baking trays, keeping them evenly spaced to allow for spreading while they bake.

Bake for 12-15 minutes, until firm to the touch. Cool on the baking trays for a few minutes, then place on a wire rack to cool completely.

For the filling, beat the peanut butter until softened. Spread the flat side of a cooled sponge half with the peanut butter.

Place another half, flat side down, on top of the filling then press both halves together.

Apple whoopie pies with cinnamon cream

Prep and cook time: 35 minutes * makes: 8

INGREDIENTS:

200 g | 7 oz | 1 cup light brown sugar
110 g | 4 oz | ½ cup butter
1 egg, beaten
225 ml | 8 fl. oz | 1 cup apple sauce
½ tsp vanilla extract
45 g | 1 ½ oz | ½ cup rolled oats
200 g | 7 oz | 1 ¾ cups plain
(all purpose) flour
1 tsp ground cinnamon
a pinch of salt
1 tsp bicarbonate of soda
(baking soda)

For the filling:
300 ml | 11 fl. oz | 1 ⅓ cups cream
1-2 tbsp icing (confectioners') sugar
1-2 tsp ground cinnamon
freshly sliced apple

METHOD:

Grind the oats in a food processor until they are a fine texture.
Preheat the oven to 180°C (160° fan) 350F, gas 4. Line 3 large
baking trays with greaseproof paper.

Beat the butter and sugar in a mixing bowl until light and
fluffy. Gradually beat in the egg, apple sauce and vanilla
until blended.

Sift in the flour, cinnamon, salt and bicarbonate of soda and
gently stir in, adding the oats, until blended.

Drop large tablespoons of the mixture onto the baking trays,
keeping them evenly spaced with enough room to spread
while baking.

Bake for 10-12 minutes, until cooked through and golden.
Cool on the baking trays for a few minutes, then place on
a wire rack to cool completely.

For the filling, whisk the cream until thick. Gradually whisk
in icing sugar and cinnamon to taste.

Add a large tablespoon of cream to a cooled sponge half.
Place another half, flat side down, on top of the filling and
gently press together.

Peppermint choc-chip whoopie pies

Prep and cook time: 35 minutes * makes: 10

INGREDIENTS:

75 g | 2 ½ oz | ⅓ cup unsalted butter
75 g | 2 ½ oz | ½ cup chopped dark
(plain) chocolate
1 large egg
150 g | 5 oz | ¾ cup dark brown sugar
125 ml | 4 ½ fl. oz | ½ cup
soured cream
25 ml | 1 fl. oz milk
1 tsp vanilla extract
¾ tsp bicarbonate of soda
(baking soda)
250 g | 9 oz | 2 ¼ cups plain
(all-purpose) flour
25 g | 1 oz | ¼ cup cocoa powder
4 tsp peppermint extract
50 g | 2 oz | ⅓ cup chocolate chips

For the filling:
100 g | 3 ½ oz white marshmallows
50 ml | 1 ¾ fl. oz milk
125 g | 4 ½ oz | ½ cup unsalted butter

METHOD:

Heat the oven to 180°C (160° fan) 350F, gas 4 and line 3 large baking trays with greaseproof paper.

Melt the butter and chocolate in a heatproof bowl over a pan of simmering water. In a separate bowl whisk the egg and sugar until thick and light. Whisk in the chocolate mixture, soured cream, milk and vanilla and peppermint extracts.

Sift in the bicarbonate of soda, flour and cocoa, stirring gently until incorporated. Stir in the chocolate chips.

Drop tablespoons of the mixture onto the baking trays. Bake for 12-15 minutes, until firm to the touch. Cool on the baking trays for a few minutes, then place on a wire rack to cool completely.

For the filling, heat the marshmallows and milk together in a pan over a low heat, stirring all the time until the marshmallows have melted and the mixture is smooth and allow it to cool slightly. Beat the butter until soft and creamy. Gradually beat the butter into the marshmallow mixture until smooth.

Spread the flat side of a cooled sponge with the filling. Place another half, flat side down, on top of the filling then press both halves together lightly.

Oaty banana whoopie pies

Prep and cook time: 40 minutes * makes: 12-15

INGREDIENTS:

50 g | 2 oz | ¼ cup butter
50 g | 2 oz | ¼ cup sugar
175 g | 6 oz | ¾ cup brown sugar
1 tbsp golden syrup (corn syrup)
1 ripe banana, mashed
½ tsp vanilla extract
120 ml | 4 fl. oz | ½ cup buttermilk
110 g | 4 oz | 1 cup plain
(all-purpose) flour
½ tsp baking powder
½ tsp bicarbonate of soda
(baking soda)
½ tsp salt
1 tsp ground cinnamon
270 g | 10 oz | 3 cups rolled oats
50 g | 2 oz | ½ cup walnuts,
finely chopped

For the filling:
100 g | 3 ½ oz | ½ cup unsalted butter
100 ml | 3 ½ fl. oz cream
½ tsp vanilla extract
350 g | 12 oz | 3 cups icing
(confectioners') sugar

METHOD:

Heat the oven to 180°C (160° fan) 350F, gas 4. Line 3 large baking trays with greaseproof paper.

Beat the butter and sugar in a mixing bowl until light and fluffy. Gradually beat in the golden syrup, banana and vanilla until blended.

In a separate bowl, sift the flour, baking powder, bicarbonate of soda, salt and cinnamon together and stir in the oats.

Slowly add the buttermilk to the flour mixture, beating well after each addition, then stir in the walnuts.

Drop tablespoonfuls of the mixture at a time onto the baking trays. Bake for10-12 minutes, until golden brown. Cool on the baking trays for a few minutes, then place on a wire rack to cool completely.

For the filling, beat the butter for 2-3 minutes until fluffy. Mix in the cream and vanilla alternately with the icing sugar, and whisk until the mixture is light and fluffy.

Spread the filling on half of the cooled sponges and sandwich together with another cooled sponge, pressing down lightly.

Milk candy whoopie pies

Prep and cook time: 50 minutes * makes: 10

INGREDIENTS:

110 g | 4 oz | ½ cup butter
180 g | 6 oz | ¾ cup caster sugar
2 eggs, beaten
350 g | 12 oz | 3 cups plain flour
1 tsp baking powder, 1 tsp vanilla extract
250 ml | 9 fl. oz | 1 cup buttermilk
pink food dye

For the filling:
225 g | 8 oz | 2 ¼ cups icing sugar
100 g | 3 ½ oz | ½ cup unsalted butter
75 g | 2 ½ oz dulce de leche
1 vanilla pod (bean)

For the fudge icing:
25 g | 1 oz | ⅛ cup butter
1 tbsp milk, 2 tsp golden syrup
1 tbsp light brown sugar
100 g | 3 ½ oz | 1 cup icing sugar

For the icing:
100 g | 3 ½ oz | 1 cup icing sugar
3-4 tsp warm water
pink food dye

METHOD:

Heat the oven to 180°C (160° fan) 350F, gas 4. Line 3 large baking trays with greaseproof paper.

Beat the butter and sugar in a mixing bowl until light and fluffy. Gradually beat in the eggs until blended.

Sift in the flour, baking powder and salt and gently stir in, adding the vanilla and buttermilk until combined. Divide the mixture in half. Stir a few drops of pink dye into 1 half.

Drop tablespoons of the mixture onto the baking trays, keeping them about 4 cm / 2 " apart.

Bake for 15 minutes, until golden. Cool on the baking trays for a few minutes, then place on a wire rack to cool completely.

For the filling, beat the butter and icing sugar with an electric whisk until smooth. Whisk in the dulce de leche. Split the vanilla pod and scrape the seeds into the mixture. Spoon the icing into a piping bag.

Pipe the icing onto the flat side of a cooled sponge and place another half, flat side down, on top of the filling, then press together.

For the icing, sift the icing sugar into a bowl and stir in just enough warm water to make a smooth, thick icing. Divide the mixture in half and colour half pink. Spread the icing on half the whoopie pies, reserving a little of the white icing for decorating.

For the fudge icing, heat the ingredients in a small pan over a low heat, stirring until combined. Allow it to cool and thicken before spreading on half the remaining whoopie pies and drizzle with the reserved white icing.

Double chocolate whoopie pies

Prep and cook time: 1 hour 5 minutes * makes: 8

INGREDIENTS:

200 g | 7 oz | 1 ¾ cups plain (all-purpose) flour
a pinch of salt
½ tsp baking powder
½ tsp bicarbonate of soda (baking soda)
45 g | 1 ½ oz | ½ cup cocoa powder
55 ml | 2 fl. oz hot milk
55 ml | 2 fl. oz hot water
175 g | 6 oz | ¾ cup light brown sugar
75 ml | 2 ½ fl. oz | ⅓ cup sunflower oil
1 egg
1 tsp vanilla extract
55 ml | 2 fl. oz buttermilk

For the filling:
200 g | 7 oz | 1 ⅓ cups chopped milk chocolate
100 ml | 3 ½ fl. oz | cream
50 g | 2 oz | ¼ cup unsalted butter

METHOD:

Heat the oven to 180°C (160° fan) 350°F gas 4. Line 3 large baking trays with greaseproof paper.

Sift the flour, salt, baking powder and bicarbonate of soda together. Put the cocoa in a separate bowl, then whisk in the hot milk and hot water until completely dissolved.

Stir the sugar and oil together until combined and then whisk into the cocoa mixture until well combined. Whisk the egg, vanilla and buttermilk into the cocoa mixture until smooth.

Gently fold the dry ingredients into the cocoa mixture, until blended. Drop tablespoons of the mixture onto the baking trays, making sure they are evenly spaced.

Bake them for 10-15 minutes, until cooked through. Insert a toothpick, if it comes out clean, the sponge halves are done. Cool on the baking trays for a few minutes, then place them on a wire rack to cool completely.

For the filling, place the chocolate, cream and butter in a heatproof bowl over a pan of simmering water. Stir until melted and smooth. Remove the bowl and set it aside to cool until it has thickened.

Spread the flat side of a cooled sponge with a generous amount of filling. Place another half, flat side down, on top of the filling then press both halves together lightly.

Strawberry marshmallow whoopie pies

Prep and cook time: 40 minutes * makes: 8

INGREDIENTS:

1 large egg

150 g | 5 oz | ¾ cup caster (superfine) sugar

75 g | 2 ½ oz | ⅓ cup unsalted butter, melted

125 ml | 4 fl. oz | ⅔ cup soured cream

1 tsp vanilla extract

275 g | 10 oz | 2 ¾ cups plain (all-purpose) flour

¾ tsp bicarbonate of soda (baking soda)

80 g | 2 ½ oz strawberry jam (jelly)

pink food dye

For the filling:

100 g | 3 ½ oz pink marshmallows

45 ml | 1 ½ fl. oz milk

½ tsp pink food dye

125 g | 4 ½ oz | ½ cup unsalted butter

METHOD:

Heat the oven to 180°C (160° fan) 350F, gas 4. Line 3 large baking trays with greaseproof paper.

Whisk the egg and sugar with an electric whisk until light and fluffy. Whisk in the melted butter, soured cream and vanilla, until combined.

Sift in the flour and bicarbonate of soda and stir in a few drops of food dye.

Drop tablespoons of the mixture onto the baking trays, keeping them about 4 cm / 2 " apart and spread them out to a 7 ½ cm / 3 " diameter.

Bake for about 15 minutes, until cooked through. Cool on the baking trays for a few minutes, then place them on a wire rack to cool completely.

For the filling, heat the marshmallows with the milk in a pan over a low heat, stirring until smooth. Stir in 1-2 drops of food dye and leave to cool for 10 minutes.

Beat the butter until creamy, then beat in the marshmallow mixture until smooth. Spread the flat side of a cooled sponge with a generous amount of filling. Place another half, flat side down, on top of the filling then gently press them together.

Red velvet vanilla whoopie pies

Prep and cook time: 45 minutes * makes: 8

INGREDIENTS:

250 g | 9 oz | 2 ¼ cups plain (all-purpose) flour

30 g | 1 oz cocoa powder

½ tsp bicarbonate of soda (baking soda)

¼ tsp salt

55 g | 2 oz | ¼ cup butter

250 g | 9 oz | 1 ¼ cups light brown sugar

1 egg

1 tsp vanilla extract

1 vanilla pod (bean)

125 ml | 4 ½ fl. oz | ½ cup buttermilk

1 tbsp red food dye

For the filling:

2 egg whites

225 g | 8 oz | 1 cup sugar

80 ml | 3 fl. oz | ⅓ cup water

1 tbsp golden syrup (corn syrup)

1 tsp vanilla extract

METHOD:

Heat the oven to 180°C (160° fan) 350F, gas 4 and line 3 large baking trays with greaseproof paper.

Mix the flour, cocoa powder, bicarbonate of soda and salt together. Beat the butter in a separate mixing bowl until soft and creamy. Beat in the sugar until light and fluffy.

Beat in the egg and vanilla until smooth. Add the flour mixture and the buttermilk, beating until just combined, then stir in the food dye. Scrape the seeds out of the vanilla pod and add them to the bowl, stirring to combine.

Drop tablespoons of the mixture onto the baking trays. Bake for 10-15 minutes, until firm to the touch. Cool on the baking trays for a few minutes, then place on a wire rack to cool completely.

For the filling, put all the ingredients in a large, heatproof bowl and whisk. Place the bowl over a pan of boiling water, then whisk constantly for 5-7 minutes or until the mixture is thick and creamy and stands in peaks. Remove from the heat, whisk for 1 minute, then it allow to cool completely.

Sandwich sponge halves together using the cream filling and gently press.

Cocoa buttermilk whoopie pies

Prep and cook time: 50 minutes ∗ makes: 12

INGREDIENTS:

125 g | 4 ½ oz | ½ cup solid
vegetable fat (shortening)
200 g | 7 oz | 1 cup dark brown sugar
1 large egg
1 tsp vanilla extract
280 g | 10 oz | 2 ¾ cups self-raising flour
40 g | 1 ½ oz | ⅓ cup cocoa powder
1 tsp baking powder
½ tsp salt
125 ml | 4 ½ fl. oz | ½ cup buttermilk
125 ml | 4 ½ fl. oz | ½ cup soured cream
100 ml | 3 ½ fl. oz hot water

For the filling:
200 g | 7 oz | 2 cups icing
(confectioners') sugar
60 g | 2 oz unsalted butter
45 ml | 1 ½ fl. oz cream
2 tsp vanilla extract
¼ tsp salt

METHOD:

Heat the oven to 180°C (160° fan) 350F, gas 4 and line 3 large baking trays with greaseproof paper.

Beat the butter and sugar in a mixing bowl with an electric whisk until light and fluffy. Gradually beat in the egg and vanilla until blended.

Sift in the flour, cocoa, baking powder and salt, then add the buttermilk and soured cream and whisk again. Add the hot water and whisk until smooth.

Put evenly spaced, large tablespoonfuls of the mixture onto the baking trays and leave to stand for 10 minutes. Bake in the oven for 10-12 minutes, until firm to the touch. Cool on the baking trays for a few minutes, then place on a wire rack to cool completely.

For the filling, sift the icing sugar into a bowl and beat in the butter until soft and creamy. Beat in the cream, vanilla and salt until the mixture is smooth.

Spread the flat side of a cooled sponge with the filling. Place another half, flat side down, on top of the filling then press both halves together lightly.

Golden syrup whoopie pies

Prep and cook time: 40 minutes * makes: 8

INGREDIENTS:

110 g | 4 oz | ½ cup butter
110 g | 4 oz | ½ cup caster
(superfine) sugar
2 eggs
1 tbsp milk
60 ml | 2 fl. oz golden syrup (corn syrup)
250 g | 9 oz | 2 ½ cups self-raising flour
1 tsp mixed spice
½ tsp salt

For the filling:
2 egg whites
225 g | 8 oz | 1 cup caster sugar
90 ml | 3 fl. oz | ⅜ cup water
1 tbsp golden syrup (corn syrup)

METHOD:

Heat the oven to 180°C (160° fan) 350F, gas 4 and line 3 large baking trays with greaseproof paper.

Beat the butter and sugar in a mixing bowl until light and fluffy. Gradually beat in the eggs, milk and syrup until blended. Sift in the flour, spice and salt and gently stir to combine.

Drop tablespoons of the mixture onto the baking trays, keeping them about 4 cm / 2 " apart.

Bake for 10-15 minutes, until golden and springy to the touch. Cool on the baking trays for a few minutes, then place on a wire rack to cool completely. For the filling, place all the ingredients in a large, heatproof bowl and whisk well.

Place the bowl over a pan of boiling water, then whisk with an electric whisk for 5-7 minutes, until the mixture is thick and creamy and stands in peaks.

Remove the bowl, whisk for 1 minute, then allow the filling to cool completely.

Spread the flat side of a cooled sponge with the filling. Place another half, flat side down, on top of the filling then gently press together.

61

Raspberry chocolate whoopie pies with mascarpone

Prep and cook time: 25 minutes * makes: 8

INGREDIENTS:

50 g | 2 oz | ¼ cup butter
75 g | 2 ½ oz | ⅓ cup caster
(superfine) sugar
1 large egg, beaten
60 g | 2 oz | ½ cup raspberries, crushed
1 tbsp cocoa powder
110 g | 4 oz | 1 cup plain
(all-purpose) flour
1 tsp bicarbonate of soda
(baking soda)

For the filling:
50 g | 2 oz | ½ cup icing
(confectioners') sugar
200 g | 7 oz | 1 cup mascarpone
few drops vanilla extract

METHOD:

Heat the oven to 200°C (180° fan) 400F, gas 6 and line 3 large baking trays with greaseproof paper.

Beat the butter and sugar in a mixing bowl until light and fluffy. Gradually beat in the egg and raspberries until blended. Sift in the cocoa, flour and baking powder and gently stir in, until smooth.

Drop tablespoons of the mixture onto the baking trays, keeping them about 4 cm / 2 " apart.

Bake for 8-10 minutes until firm to the touch. Cool on the baking trays for a few minutes, then place on a wire rack to cool completely.

For the filling, sift the icing sugar into a bowl and gradually beat in the mascarpone and vanilla until smooth.

Spread the flat side of a cooled sponge with the filling. Place another half, flat side down, on top of the filling then press both halves together lightly.

Chocolate whoopie pies with rhubarb and strawberry compote

Prep and cook time: 40 minutes * makes: 8

INGREDIENTS:

200 g | 7 oz | 1 ¾ cups plain (all-purpose) flour
a pinch of salt
½ tsp baking powder
½ tsp bicarbonate of soda (baking soda)
45 g | 1 ½ oz | ½ cup cocoa powder
110 ml | 4 fl. oz hot water
175 g | 6 oz | ¾ cup light brown sugar
75 ml | 2 ½ fl. oz | ⅓ cup sunflower oil
1 egg
1 tsp vanilla extract
55 ml | 2 fl. oz buttermilk

For the filling:
450 g | 1 lb | 2 cups sugar
600 ml | 21 fl. oz | 2 ½ cups water
450 g | 1 lb rhubarb, sliced
400 g | 14 oz | 2 cups sliced strawberries

METHOD:

Heat the oven to 180°C (160° fan) 350F, gas 4. Line 3 large baking trays with greaseproof paper.

Sift the flour, salt, baking powder and bicarbonate of soda together. In a separate bowl, whisk the cocoa and hot water together until completely dissolved.

Stir the sugar and oil together until combined and then whisk into the cocoa mixture until smooth. Whisk the egg, vanilla and buttermilk into the cocoa mixture until smooth.

Gently fold the dry ingredients into the cocoa mixture, until blended. Drop tablespoonfuls of the mixture onto the baking trays, keeping them evenly spaced.

Bake for 10-15 minutes, until cooked through. Cool on the trays for a few minutes, then place on a wire rack to cool completely.

For the filling, heat the sugar and water in a pan until the sugar has dissolved, increase the heat to boiling point for a few minutes.

Add the rhubarb to the syrup and increase the heat to boiling point. Simmer for 2 minutes and remove it from the heat, and allow the rhubarb to cool completely. Add the strawberries to the rhubarb and chill until you are ready to assemble the whoopie pies.

Place a spoonful of the rhubarb and strawberry compote on the flat side of a cold sponge pie. Top with a scoop of ice-cream. Place another half, flat side down, on top of the filling then press both halves together lightly.

Top each whoopie pie with a scoop of ice-cream and spoon a little fruit compote around each whoopie pie.

Chocolate whoopie pies with lemon buttercream

Prep and cook time: 35 minutes * makes: 10

INGREDIENTS:

225 g | 8 oz | 1 cup sugar
90 ml | 3 fl. oz sunflower oil
2 eggs
225 g | 8 oz | 2 cups plain
(all-purpose) flour
50 g | 2 oz | ½ cup cocoa powder
1 tsp bicarbonate of soda
(baking soda)
½ tsp salt
60 ml | 2 fl. oz milk

For the filling:
175 g | 6 oz | ¾ cup unsalted butter
175 g | 6 oz | 1 ¾ cups icing
(confectioners') sugar
45 g | 1 ½ oz lemon curd
2-3 tsp lemon juice

To decorate:
110 g | 4 oz | ¾ cup chopped milk chocolate
chocolate sprinkles

METHOD:

Heat the oven to 200°C (180° fan) 400F, gas 6 and line 3 large baking trays with greaseproof paper. Beat the sugar and oil in a mixing bowl until crumbly. Gradually beat in the eggs until blended.

Sift in the flour, cocoa, bicarbonate of soda and salt and beat well. Stir in the vanilla and milk to form a very soft dough.

With lightly floured hands, roll the dough into 3 cm / 1 ½ " balls. Place the balls 5 cm / 2 " apart on the baking trays and flatten them slightly.

Bake for 5-8 minutes, until the tops are cracked. Cool on the baking trays for a few minutes, then place them on a wire rack to cool completely.

For the filling, beat the butter until soft and creamy. Sift in the icing sugar and beat well. Add the lemon curd and lemon juice to taste and beat until smooth. Put the buttercream into a piping bag.

Pipe buttercream onto the flat side of a cooled sponge. Place another half, flat side down, on top of the filling then press both halves together lightly.

To decorate, melt the chocolate in a heatproof bowl over a pan of simmering water. Allow it to cool slightly and then spread it over the top of the whoopie pies. Add the sprinkles before the chocolate sets.

Mini lemon whoopie pies

Prep and cook time: 30 minutes * makes: 20

INGREDIENTS:

110 g | 4 oz | ½ cup butter
110 g | 4 oz | ½ cup caster
(superfine) sugar
2 eggs
1 lemon, juice and zest
225 g | 8 oz | 2 cups self-raising flour
½ tsp salt

For the filling:
75 g | 2 ½ oz | ⅜ cup butter
175 g | 6 oz | ¾ cup cream cheese
1 lemon, zest
225 g | 8 oz | 2 ¼ cups icing
(confectioners') sugar

METHOD:

Heat the oven to 180°C (160° fan) 350F, gas 4 and line
3 large baking trays with greaseproof paper.

Beat the butter and sugar in a mixing bowl until light and fluffy.
Gradually beat in the eggs, lemon juice and zest until blended.

Sift in the flour and salt and gently stir in until smooth.
Drop heaped teaspoons of the mixture onto the baking trays.
Bake for about 12-15 minutes, until cooked through. Cool the
sponge halves on the baking trays for a few minutes, then
place on a wire rack to cool completely.

For the filling, beat the butter, cream cheese and lemon zest
together, then sift in the icing sugar and beat the mixture
until smooth.

Spread the flat side of a cooled sponge half with the filling.
Place another half, flat side down, on top of the filling then
press both halves together lightly.

Rosa Whoopie Pies

Prep and cook time: 40 minutes * makes: 10

INGREDIENTS:

350 g | 12 oz | 3 ½ cups plain
(all-purpose) flour
1 ½ tsp baking powder
1 tsp bicarbonate of soda
(baking soda)
½ tsp salt
400 g | 14 oz | 2 cups caster
(superfine) sugar
150 g | 5 oz | ¾ cup butter, melted
110 ml | 4 fl. oz | ½ cup plain yoghurt
2 large eggs
1 tsp raspberry extract
pink food dye

For the filling and topping:
225 g | 8 oz | 1 cup unsalted
butter, softened
450 g | 1 lb | 4 ½ cups icing
(confectioners') sugar
120 ml | 4 fl. oz cream
2 tsp vanilla extract
pink sprinkles

METHOD:

Heat the oven to 180°C (160° fan) 350F, gas 4. Line 3 large
baking trays with greaseproof paper.

Mix the flour, baking powder, bicarbonate of soda and salt
together. Whisk the sugar and butter in a mixing bowl until
smooth, then whisk in the yoghurt until blended.

Gradually whisk in the eggs, raspberry extract and a few drops
of food dye. Gently fold in the flour mixture until smooth.
Drop tablespoons of the mixture onto the baking trays,
making sure they are evenly spaced.

Bake for about 15 minutes, until cooked through. Insert a
toothpick, if it comes out clean the cakes are done. Cool on the
baking trays for a few minutes, then place on a wire rack
to cool completely.

For the filling and topping, beat the butter until creamy. Sift in
the icing sugar and vanilla and beat until smooth. In a separate
bowl, whip the cream until it is stiffly peaking, then add it to the
butter mixture.

Spread the flat side of a cooled sponge with the filling. Place
another half, flat side down, on top of the filling then press
both halves together lightly. Spread the remaining mixture
on top of the whoopie pies and scatter with sprinkles.

Passion fruit and pumpkin whoopie pies

Prep and cook time: 30 minutes * makes: 8

INGREDIENTS:

110 g | 4 oz | ½ cup unsalted butter, melted

200 g | 7 oz | 1 cup light brown sugar

2 large eggs, beaten

225 g | 8 oz | 1 cup canned pumpkin puree

200 g | 7 oz | 1 ¾ cups plain (all-purpose) flour

1 tsp mixed spice

¼ tsp grated nutmeg

¼ tsp ground cinnamon

1 tsp vanilla extract

1 tsp baking powder

1 tsp bicarbonate of soda (baking soda)

½ tsp salt

For the filling:

200 g | 7 oz | 1 cup mascarpone

75 ml | 2 ½ fl. oz | ⅓ cup cream

30 g | 1 oz icing (confectioners') sugar

3 passion fruit, pulp and seeds

METHOD:

Heat the oven to 180°C (160° fan) 350F, gas 4. Line 2 large baking trays with greaseproof paper.

Whisk the melted butter and sugar together in a mixing bowl until smooth. Whisk in the eggs, pumpkin puree, spices and vanilla.

Sift in the baking powder, bicarbonate of soda, salt and flour and gently stir.

Drop tablespoons of the mixture onto the baking trays. Bake them for about 10 minutes, until they are golden brown and springy to the touch. Cool on the baking trays for a few minutes, then place on a wire rack to cool completely.

For the filling, whisk the mascarpone, cream and icing sugar until the mixture begins to thicken. Add the passion fruit pulp and seeds and beat until firm.

Spread the filling on half of the sponge halves. Top with the remaining halves and press together.

Pink whoopie pies

Prep and cook time: 40 minutes * makes: 12

INGREDIENTS:

125 g | 4 ½ oz | ½ cup butter
200 g | 7 oz | 1 cup caster
(superfine) sugar
1 egg, beaten
400 g | 14 oz | 3 ½ cups plain
(all-purpose) flour
1 ¼ tsp bicarbonate of soda
(baking soda)
½ tsp salt
1 tsp vanilla extract
250 ml | 9 fl. oz | 1 cup buttermilk

For the filling:
200 g | 7 oz | 1 cup sliced strawberries
30 g | 1 oz icing (confectioners') sugar
300 ml | 11 fl. oz | 1 ⅓ cups cream

To decorate:
175 g | 6 oz | 1 ¾ cups icing sugar
1-2 tbsp water
50 g | 2 oz white chocolate shavings

METHOD:

Heat the oven to 180°C (160° fan) 350F, gas 4 and line 3 large
baking trays with greaseproof paper.

Beat the butter and sugar in a mixing bowl until light and fluffy.
Gradually beat in the egg until blended.

Sift in the flour, bicarbonate of soda and salt and gently stir in.
Add the vanilla and buttermilk until smooth and thick, you may
not need all the buttermilk.

Drop tablespoons of the mixture onto the baking trays, about
4 cm / 2 " apart.

Bake for 10-15 minutes, until cooked through. Cool the sponge
halves on the baking trays for a few minutes, then place on a wire
rack to cool completely.

For the filling, purée the strawberries in a food processor or with
a hand-held blender. Pass the purée through a sieve and stir in
the icing sugar. Whisk the cream until stiff and fold it into the
strawberry purée. Put the strawberry cream into a piping bag.

Pipe swirls of the filling onto the flat side of a cooled sponge half.
Place another half, flat side down, on top of the filling then gently
press together.

For the icing, sift the icing sugar into a bowl and gradually beat
in enough water to give a smooth, thick icing. Spread the icing
over the top of the whoopie pies. Decorate with chocolate shavings
before the icing sets.

Chocolate whoopie pies with lemon cream

Prep and cook time: 35 minutes * makes: 6

INGREDIENTS:

35 g | 1 ¼ oz | ¼ cup cocoa powder
300 g | 11 oz | 2 ½ cups plain
(all-purpose) flour
1 tsp bicarbonate of soda
(baking soda)
1 tsp baking powder
a pinch of salt
110 g | 4 oz | ½ cup unsalted butter
175 g | 6 oz | ¾ cup dark brown sugar
1 egg
1 tsp vanilla extract
125 ml | 4 ½ fl. oz | ½ cup milk

For the filling:
300 ml | 11 fl. oz | 1 ⅓ cups cream
1 lemon, zest
50 g | 2 oz | ½ cup icing
(confectioners') sugar
50 g | 2 oz lemon jelly sweets,
finely chopped

METHOD:

Heat the oven to 160°C (140° fan) 325F, gas 3 and line 2 large baking trays with greaseproof paper.

Sift the cocoa, flour, bicarbonate of soda, baking powder and salt together. Beat the butter and sugar in a mixing bowl until light and fluffy. Gradually beat in the egg until blended.

Gently beat the vanilla and milk together. Add the cocoa and flour mixture to the butter mixture, adding the milk mixture and beating until smooth.

Spoon the batter into mounds onto the baking trays, spacing them about 4 cm / 2 " apart.

Bake the whoopie pies for about 15 minutes, until firm to the touch. Cool them on the baking trays for a few minutes, then place on a wire rack to cool completely.

For the filling, whisk the cream until it is thick. Stir in the lemon zest and sift in the icing sugar, then stir in the lemon jelly sweets.

Spread the flat side of a cooled cake with a generous amount of filling. Place another half, flat side down, on top of the filling then press both halves together lightly.

Red velvet whoopie pies

Prep and cook time: 40 minutes * makes: 8

INGREDIENTS:

125 g | 4 ½ oz | ½ cup butter
175 g | 6 oz | ¾ cup sugar
1 egg
300 g | 11 oz | 2 ½ cups plain
(all-purpose) flour
a pinch of salt
1 ½ tsp bicarbonate of soda
(baking soda)
250 ml | 9 fl. oz | 1 cup buttermilk
25 g | 1 oz | ¼ cup cocoa powder
1 tsp red dye paste

For the filling:
2 egg whites
140 g | 5 oz | ⅔ cup sugar
1 tsp vanilla extract
220 g | 8 oz | 1 cup unsalted butter

METHOD:

Heat the oven to 180°C (160° fan) 350F, gas 4 and line 3 large baking trays with greaseproof paper.

Beat the butter and sugar in a mixing bowl until light and fluffy. Gradually beat in the egg until blended.

Sift in the flour, salt and bicarbonate of soda and gently stir in with the buttermilk, until smooth.

Mix the cocoa powder and red dye paste together and stir into the mixture, until thoroughly combined.

Drop tablespoons of the mixture at a time onto the baking trays, keeping them evenly spaced.

Bake for 10-15 minutes, until springy to the touch. Cool the sponge halves on the baking trays for a few minutes, then place them on a wire rack to cool completely.

For the filling, whisk the egg whites in a heatproof bowl until foamy. Mix in the sugar and place the bowl over a pan of simmering water. Whisk until the mixture is piping hot and the sugar has dissolved.

Remove the bowl and whisk in the vanilla. Gradually whisk in the butter until the mixture is smooth and thick, then allow it to cool.

Spread the flat side of a cooled sponge with a generous amount of filling. Place another half, flat side down, on top of the filling then gently press together.

Peppermint cream whoopie pies

Prep and cook time: 40 minutes * makes: 12

INGREDIENTS:

35 g | 1 ¼ oz | ¼ cup cocoa powder
300 g | 11 oz | 2 ¾ cups plain
(all-purpose) flour
1 tsp bicarbonate of soda
(baking soda)
1 tsp baking powder
a pinch of salt
100 g | 3 ½ oz | ½ cup unsalted butter
175 g | 6 oz | ¾ cup dark muscovado sugar
1 egg
1 tsp vanilla extract
125 ml | 4 ½ fl. oz | ½ cup milk
2 tsp peppermint extract

For the filling:
200 g | 7 oz | 2 cups icing
(confectioners') sugar
60 g | 2 oz unsalted butter
30 ml | 1 fl. oz cream
1 tsp peppermint extract

METHOD:

Heat the oven to 170°C (150° fan) 325F, gas 3 and line 3 large baking trays with greaseproof paper.

Sift the cocoa, flour, bicarbonate of soda, baking powder, and salt together. In a separate bowl, beat the butter, sugar and egg together until smooth and light.

Add the cocoa mixture to the egg mixture, followed by the milk, vanilla and peppermint extract and beat until smooth.

Spoon the batter into mounds onto the baking trays, keeping them about 4 cm / 2 " apart.

Bake for about 15 minutes, until firm to the touch. Cool them on the baking trays for a few minutes, then place on a wire rack to cool completely.

For the filling, sift the icing sugar into a bowl and beat in the butter until soft and creamy. Beat in the cream and peppermint extract until the mixture is smooth.

Spread the flat side of a cold cake with the filling. Place another half, flat side down, on top of the filling then press both halves together lightly.

Violet whoopie pies

Prep and cook time: 35 minutes * makes: 8

INGREDIENTS:

110 g | 4 oz | ½ cup butter
200 g | 7 oz | 1 cup caster
(superfine) sugar
1 large egg, beaten
1 tsp violet liqueur
½ tsp purple food dye
400 g | 14 oz | 3 ½ cups plain
(all-purpose) flour
¼ tsp bicarbonate of soda
(baking soda)
½ tsp salt
225 ml | 8 fl. oz | 1 cup buttermilk

For the filling:
300 ml | 11 fl. oz | 1 ⅓ cups cream
2-3 tbsp icing (confectioners') sugar

METHOD:

Heat the oven to 180°C (160° fan) 350F, gas 4 and line 3 large baking trays with greaseproof paper.

Beat the butter and sugar in a mixing bowl until light and fluffy. Gradually beat in the egg, liqueur and food dye until blended.

Sift in the dry ingredients and stir gently until the mixture is smooth. Stir in the buttermilk until the mixture is smooth and thick.

Drop tablespoons of the mixture onto the baking trays, keeping them evenly spaced with enough room to spread as they bake.

Bake for 12-15 minutes, until firm to the touch. Cool on the baking trays for a few minutes, then place them on a wire rack to cool completely.

For the filling, whisk the cream and icing sugar until thick. Spread the filling on the flat side of a cold cake. Place another half on top of the filling and gently press together.

Classic red velvet whoopie pies

Prep and cook time: 1 hour ∗ makes: 8

INGREDIENTS:

125 g | 4 ½ oz | ½ cup butter
180 g | 6 oz | ¾ cup light brown sugar
1 egg
300 g | 11 oz | 2 ½ cups plain
(all-purpose) flour
½ tsp salt
1 ½ tsp bicarbonate of soda
(baking soda)
250 ml | 9 fl. oz | 1 cup buttermilk
25 g | 1 oz | ¼ cup cocoa powder
1 tsp red dye paste

For the filling:
225 g | 8 oz | 1 cup cream cheese
45 g | 1 ½ oz unsalted butter
250 g | 9 oz | 2 ½ cups icing
(confectioners') sugar
1 tsp vanilla extract

METHOD:

Heat the oven to 180°C (160° fan) 350F, gas 4 and line 3 large baking trays with greaseproof paper.

Beat the butter and sugar in a mixing bowl until light and fluffy. Gradually beat in the egg until blended.

In a separate bowl, mix the flour, salt and bicarbonate of soda together. In another bowl, blend the cocoa powder with the red dye paste.

Add the flour mixture to the butter mixture add follow with the buttermilk. Mix in the red cocoa powder mixture until smooth and blended.

Drop tablespoons of the mixture at a time onto the baking trays, roughly 7 ½ cm / 3 " in diameter.

Bake for 10-15 minutes, until firm to the touch. Cool on the baking trays for a few minutes, then place on a wire rack to cool completely.

For the filling, whisk the cream cheese and butter with an electric whisk until smooth and creamy. Sift in the icing sugar and whisk until well blended and stir in the vanilla. Chill the cream for 30 minutes before using.

Spread the flat side of a cooled sponge with a generous amount of filling. Place another half, flat side down, on top of the filling then gently press the two halves together.

Strawberry and vanilla whoopie pies

Prep and cook time: 35 minutes * makes: 8

INGREDIENTS:

110 g | 4 oz | ½ cup butter
200 g | 7 oz | 1 cup caster
(superfine) sugar
1 large egg, beaten
1 tsp strawberry extract
½ tsp pink food dye
400 g | 14 oz | 3 ½ cups plain
(all-purpose) flour
¼ tsp bicarbonate of soda
(baking soda)
½ tsp salt
225 ml | 8 fl. oz | 1 cup buttermilk

For the filling:
150 g | 5 oz | ½ cup unsalted butter
250 g | 9 oz | 2 ½ cups icing
(confectioners') sugar
1 tsp vanilla extract

METHOD:

Heat the oven to 180°C (160° fan) 350F, gas 4. Line 3 large baking trays with greaseproof paper.

Beat the butter and sugar in a mixing bowl until light and fluffy. Gradually beat in the egg, strawberry extract and food dye until smooth and blended.

Sift in the dry ingredients and stir gently until combined. Stir in the buttermilk until the mixture is smooth and thick.

Drop tablespoons of the mixture onto the baking trays, so they are roughly 7 ½ cm / 3 " in diameter.

Bake for 12-15 minutes, until firm to the touch. Cool the sponge halves on the baking trays for a few minutes, then place on a wire rack to cool completely.

For the filling, beat the butter until soft, then sift in the icing sugar and beat until smooth. Stir in the vanilla.

Sandwich the sponge halves, flat sides together, with the vanilla cream filling and gently press. Leave the filling to set for at least 30 minutes before serving.

Raspberry cream whoopie pies

Prep and cook time: 40 minutes ∗ makes: 8

INGREDIENTS:

110 g | 4 oz | ½ cup butter
110 g | 4 oz | ½ cup caster
(superfine) sugar
2 eggs
250 g | 9 oz | 2 ½ cups self-raising flour
½ tsp salt
1 tsp rosewater
110 ml | 4 fl. oz milk
2 tsp red food dye

For the filling:
100 g | 3 ½ oz | 1 cup raspberries
30 g | 1 oz icing (confectioners') sugar
1 tbsp lemon juice
400 ml | 14 fl. oz | 1 ⅔ cups cream
pink food dye

For the icing:
175 g | 6 oz | 1 ¾ cups icing sugar
1-2 tbsp water
pink food dye

METHOD:

Heat the oven to 180°C (160° fan) 350F, gas 4. Line 3 large baking trays with greaseproof paper.

Beat the butter and sugar in a mixing bowl until light and fluffy and gradually beat in the eggs. Sift in the flour and salt and gently stir in, until combined. Stir in the rosewater and milk.

Drop tablespoons of the mixture onto the baking trays, keeping them at least 4 cm / 2 " apart and spread out a little to 7 ½ cm / 3 " diameter rounds.

Bake for about 15 minutes, until cooked through. Cool them on the baking trays for a few minutes, then place on a wire rack to cool completely.

For the filling, puree the raspberries and sugar in a food processor or blender. Push the mixture through a sieve into a bowl and stir in the lemon juice. Whisk the cream until stiff and stir in the raspberry mixture and a few drops of food dye.

Sandwich the sponge halves together using the raspberry cream filling.

For the icing, sift the icing sugar into a bowl and gradually beat in enough water to give a smooth, thick icing. Stir in a few drops of food dye. Drizzle the icing over the top of the whoopie pies.

Whoopie pies with raspberries

Prep and cook time: 40 minutes * makes: 10-12

INGREDIENTS:

110 g | 4 oz | ½ cup butter
225 g | 8 oz | 1 cup sugar
1 egg, beaten
½ tsp vanilla extract
250 g | 9 oz | 2 ¼ cups plain
(all-purpose) flour
1 ½ tsp baking powder
¼ tsp salt
150 ml | 5 fl. oz | ⅔ cup milk
110 g | 4 oz | 1 cup raspberries, crushed
pink food dye

For the filling:
175 g | 6 oz | ¾ cup unsalted butter
100 g | 3 ½ oz | 1 cup icing
(confectioners') sugar
¼ tsp vanilla extract
100 g | 3 ½ oz marshmallow cream
1 tbsp cream

To decorate:
175 g | 6 oz | 1 ¾ cups icing sugar
1-2 tbsp water
pink food dye

METHOD:

Heat the oven to 180°C (160° fan) 350F, gas 4 and line 3 large baking trays with greaseproof paper.

Beat the butter and sugar in a mixing bowl until light and fluffy. Gradually beat in the egg and vanilla until blended.

Sift in the flour, baking powder and salt and gently stir in until combined. Stir in the milk and raspberries until blended, then stir in a few drops of pink food dye.

Drop large tablespoons of the mixture onto the baking trays. Bake for 10-15 minutes, until springy to the touch. Cool on the baking trays for a few minutes, then place on a wire rack to cool completely.

For the filling, beat the butter and icing sugar until light and fluffy. Add the vanilla, marshmallow cream and cream and beat well until smooth.

Spread the flat side of a cooled sponge with the filling. Place another half, flat side down, on top of the filling then press both halves together.

To decorate, sift the icing sugar into a bowl and gradually beat in enough water to give a smooth, thick icing. Stir in the food dye until blended. Drizzle or pipe the icing over the top of the whoopie pies.

Cherry almond whoopie pies

Prep and cook time: 50 minutes * makes: 12

INGREDIENTS:

125 g | 4 ½ oz | ½ cup unsalted butter

200 g | 7 oz | 1 cup caster (superfine) sugar

1 egg, beaten

400 g | 14 oz | 3 ½ cups plain (all-purpose) flour

1 ¼ tsp bicarbonate of soda (baking soda)

½ tsp salt

270 ml | 10 fl. oz | 1 ⅛ cups buttermilk

1 tsp almond extract

100 g | 3 ½ oz | ½ cup glace (candied) cherries, chopped

50 g | 2 oz | ¾ cup almonds, chopped

For the filling:

250 g | 9 oz white mini marshmallows

1 tbsp water

METHOD:

Heat the oven to 180°C (160°C fan) 375°F, gas 5. Heat the oven to 160°C (140° fan) 325F, gas 3 and line 3 large baking trays with greaseproof paper.

Beat the butter and sugar in a mixing bowl until light and fluffy. Gradually beat in the egg so the mixture doesn't curdle.

Sift in the flour, bicarbonate of soda and salt and gently stir in, alternately with the buttermilk, until smooth. Stir in the almond extract, cherries and almonds.

Drop tablespoons of mixture onto the baking trays, making sure they are evenly spaced so they can spread while baking.

Bake for 10-15 minutes, until cooked through. Cool the sponge halves on the baking trays for a few minutes, then place on a wire rack to cool completely.

For the filling, put the marshmallows and water into a pan and gently heat until melted. Stir well and leave to cool for 20 minutes until sticky.

Spoon the flat side of a cold cake with a generous amount of filling. Place another half, flat side down, on top of the filling then gently press the two halves together.

Blueberry and sour cream whoopie pies

Prep and cook time: 35 minutes * makes: 12

INGREDIENTS:

225 g | 8 oz | 2 cups plain
(all-purpose) flour
1 tsp ground cinnamon
½ tsp bicarbonate of soda
(baking soda)
¼ tsp salt
175 g | 6 oz | ¾ cup butter
225 g | 8 oz | 1 cup sugar
1 large egg
120 ml | 4 fl. oz | ½ cup soured cream
100 g | 3 ½ oz | 1 cup blueberries

For the filling:
400 ml | 14 fl. oz | 1 ⅔ cups cream
30 g | 1 oz icing (confectioners') sugar

METHOD:

Heat the oven to 180°C (160° fan) 350F, gas 4. Line 3 large
baking trays with greaseproof paper.

Sift the flour, cinnamon, bicarbonate of soda and salt together
and set the bowl aside. Beat the butter and sugar in a mixing
bowl until light and fluffy. Gradually beat in the egg until blended.

Combine the contents of the bowls and then stir in the soured
cream and blueberries. Drop heaped tablespoons of the mixture
onto the baking trays.

Bake for 9-12 minutes, until golden and cooked through.
Insert a toothpick, if it comes out clean, they are done. Cool on
the baking trays for a few minutes, then place on a wire rack
to cool completely.

For the filling, whisk the cream until thick. Sift in the icing sugar
and whisk until smooth.

Sandwich two sponge halves together using the cream filling and
gently press down.

COOKIES.

Oatmeal raisin cookies

Prep and cook time: 25 minutes * makes: 20-24

INGREDIENTS:

100 g | 3 ½ oz | ½ cup butter
100 g | 3 ½ oz | ½ cup caster
(superfine) sugar
30 ml | 1 fl. oz honey
2 eggs
1 tsp ground cinnamon
100 g | 3 ½ oz | 1 cup wholemeal flour
1 tsp baking powder
80 g | 3 oz | 1 cup rolled oats
50 g | 2 oz | ½ cup raisins
50 g | 2 oz | ½ cup dried cranberries

METHOD:

Heat the oven to 180°C (160° fan) 350F, gas 4 and lightly grease a large baking tray with oil.

Beat the butter and sugar in a mixing bowl until soft, then beat in the honey.

Add the egg and cinnamon and mix well. Stir in the flour, baking powder, oats, raisins and cranberries until everything is combined.

Drop spoonfuls of the mixture onto the baking tray and bake for 10-12 minutes, until lightly golden.

Cool the cookies on the baking tray for a few minutes, then place them on a wire rack to cool completely.

Shortbread

Prep and cook time: 50 minutes * makes: 10

INGREDIENTS:

225 g | 8 oz | 2 cups plain
(all-purpose) flour
110 g | 4 oz | ¾ cup rice flour
110 g | 4 oz | 1 cup icing
(confectioners') sugar
225 g | 8 oz | 1 cup unsalted butter
caster (superfine) sugar, to decorate

METHOD:

Heat the oven to 150°C (130° fan) 300F, gas 2.

Line a large baking tray with greaseproof paper. Sift the flour,
rice flour and icing sugar into a mixing bowl. Knead in the butter
and mix to a soft dough.

Roll out the dough on a lightly floured surface about 2 ½ cm /
1 " thick. Cut out rounds and place on the baking tray.

Bake for 25-35 minutes, until cooked but still pale. Sprinkle with
caster sugar while still warm. Cool on the baking tray for 10 minutes,
then carefully remove and place on a wire rack to cool completely.

Chocolate chip cookies

Prep and cook time: 25 minutes * makes: 30

INGREDIENTS:

150 g | 5 oz | ¾ cup butter
150 g | 5 oz | ¾ cup light brown sugar
1 egg
1 tsp vanilla extract
300 g | 11 oz | 2 ¾ cups plain
(all-purpose) flour
½ tsp baking powder
100 g | 3 ½ oz | ½ cup dark (plain)
chocolate chips
100 g | 3 ½ oz | ½ cup white
chocolate chips

METHOD:

Beat the butter and sugar in a mixing bowl, then mix in the egg and vanilla.

Stir in half the flour and then the chocolate chips. Stir until the chocolate is well mixed, then add the remaining flour until a smooth cookie batter has formed. Form the batter into a dough ball.

Heat the oven to 190°C (170° fan) 375F, gas 5 and line a large baking tray with greaseproof paper.

Cut the dough into 30 pieces. Roll it into balls and place them onto the baking tray to bake for 7 minutes. Remove the cookies from the oven and press each ball with the back of a spoon, until they slightly spread. Return the cookies to the oven for a further 7 minutes, until browned.

Cool the cookies on the baking trays for a few minutes, then place on a wire rack to cool completely.

Cream-filled chocolate biscuits

Prep and cook time: 1 hour 45 minutes * makes: 30

INGREDIENTS:

300 g | 11 oz dark (plain) chocolate
100 g | 3 ½ oz | ½ cup butter
3 eggs
250 g | 9 oz | 1 ¼ cups sugar
100 g | 3 ½ oz | ¾ cup plain
(all-purpose) flour
1 tsp baking powder
a pinch of salt
2-3 tbsp ground hazelnuts

For the filling:
200 ml | 7 fl. oz | ⅞ cup soured cream
100 g | 3 ½ oz | 1 cup icing
(confectioners) sugar
100 ml | 3 ½ fl. oz cream

For the icing:
250 g | 9 oz hazelnut chocolate spread
1 tbsp oil

METHOD:

Heat the oven to 160°C (140° fan) 325F, gas 3 and line a large baking tray with greaseproof paper.

Melt the chocolate with the butter in a heatproof bowl over a pan of simmering water.

Beat the eggs and sugar until creamy. Mix the flour, baking powder and salt together. Fold the dry ingredients into the chocolate butter and add the ground hazelnuts.

Place teaspoonfuls of the dough on the baking tray and make a slight indentation in the middle of each. Bake for about 8 minutes until firm. Cool the biscuits on the baking trays for a few minutes, then place on a wire rack to cool completely.

Beat the soured cream until smooth with half of the icing sugar. Whisk the cream until thick, with a teaspoon of icing sugar. Fold the whipped cream into the soured cream and sweeten with the remaining icing sugar if desired. Place a teaspoon of cream in the centre of each cookie and chill.

Melt the hazelnut spread with the oil, as before and spread over the cream on each cookie.

Walnut biscuits

Prep and cook time: 35 minutes * makes: 15-20

INGREDIENTS:

75 ml | 2 ½ fl. oz walnut oil
110 g | 4 oz | ½ cup butter
150 g | 5 oz | ¾ cup light brown sugar
225 g | 8 oz | 2 cups self raising flour
¼ tsp salt
1 egg, beaten
110 g | 4 oz | 1 cup walnut halves

METHOD:

Heat the oven to 190°C (170° fan) 375F, gas 5 and line 2 large baking trays with greaseproof paper.

Cream the walnut oil and butter together until smooth. Stir in the sugar, flour, salt and walnuts. Bind with enough egg to form a soft dough.

Form the dough into a roll and wrap it in cling film. Chill the dough for at least 4 hours, or overnight, until firm.

Slice the roll into rounds with a sharp knife and place on the baking trays.

Bake the cookies for 10-15 minutes until crisp and golden. Cool on the baking trays for a few minutes, then place them on a wire rack to cool completely.

Orange and hazelnut stars

Prep and cook time: 1 hour 30 minutes * makes: 20

INGREDIENTS:

80 g | 3 oz | ⅓ cup butter

100 g | 3 ½ oz | ½ cup sugar

250 g | 9 oz | 1 ½ cups plain
(all-purpose) flour

½ tsp baking powder

1 egg

1 orange, zest

30 ml | 1 fl. oz orange juice

175 g | 6 oz | 1 cup chopped
white chocolate

175 g | 6 oz | 1 cup chopped hazelnuts
(cobnuts), lightly crushed

150 g | 5 oz | ½ cup orange marmalade

METHOD:

Heat the oven to 180°C (160° fan) 350F, gas 4. Line a large
baking tray with greaseproof paper.

Beat the butter and sugar in a mixing bowl. Sift in the flour
and baking powder until combined.

Beat in the egg, orange zest and juice and mix to a dough.
Shape into a ball, wrap in cling film and chill for 1 hour.

Roll out the dough thinly on a lightly floured surface. Cut out
stars and place them on the baking tray. Bake for 12-15 minutes
until golden. Cool on the baking tray for a few minutes, then
place on a wire rack to cool completely.

Melt the chocolate in a heatproof bowl over a pan of simmering
water. Dip half of the biscuits in the chocolate, to coat one side.
Sprinkle with hazelnut sprinkles and leave to set.

Sandwich the coated and non-coated biscuits together
with orange marmalade.

White chocolate biscuits

Prep and cook time: 25 minutes * makes: 30

INGREDIENTS:

225 g | 8 oz | 1 cup butter
225 g | 8 oz | 1 cup caster
(superfine) sugar
½ tsp vanilla extract
170 ml | 6 fl. oz | ¾ cup
condensed milk
350 g | 12 oz | 3 cups self-raising flour
150 g | 5 oz white chocolate,
roughly chopped

METHOD:

Heat the oven to 180°C (160° fan) 350F, gas 4. Line 2 baking trays with greaseproof paper.

Beat the butter and sugar in a mixing bowl until pale and then stir in the vanilla and condensed milk.

Sift in the flour and work to a soft dough with your hands. Mix in the chocolate.

Roll small pieces of dough into balls and place well apart on the baking trays. Flatten with your fingers.

Bake for 15-18 minutes, until golden brown at the edges, but still a little soft.

Cool on the baking trays for a few minutes, then place on a wire rack to cool completely.

Peanut butter cookies

Prep and cook time: 30 minutes * makes: 30-40

INGREDIENTS:

310 g | 11 oz | 2 ½ cups plain (all-purpose) flour
½ tsp bicarbonate of soda (baking soda)
½ tsp baking powder
1 tsp salt
240 g | 8 oz | 1 cup unsalted butter, softened
210 g | 7 oz | 1 ⅓ cups light brown sugar
210 g | 7 oz | 1 cup granulated sugar
270 g | 10 oz | 1 cup extra crunchy peanut butter
2 large eggs
2 tsp vanilla extract
140 g | 5 oz | 1 cup ground dry-roasted peanuts

METHOD:

Heat the oven to 180°C (160° fan) 350F gas 4 and line 2 baking trays with greaseproof paper.

Sift the flour, bicarbonate of soda, baking powder and salt together then set it aside.

Beat the butter until creamy, then add the sugars and beat until fluffy the mixture is smooth and fluffy.

Add the peanut butter until combined and then add the eggs. Add the vanilla and gently stir in the dry ingredients and the ground peanuts.

Roll the dough into 5 cm / 2 " balls. Place the balls on the baking trays, spacing them evenly. Press a fork into each dough ball twice to make a criss-cross design.

Bake for 10-12 minutes until risen and slightly brown around the edges.

Cool the biscuits on the baking trays for a few minutes, then place on a wire rack to cool completely.

Chocolate hazelnut meringues

Prep and cook time: 1 hour * makes: 30

INGREDIENTS:

6 egg whites
300 g | 11 oz | 2 ½ cups caster (superfine) sugar
50 g | 2 oz | ½ cup dark chocolate, grated
1 tsp white wine vinegar
150 g | 5 oz | ¾ cup roasted hazelnuts (cobnuts), chopped

METHOD:

Heat the oven to 180°C (160° fan) 350F, gas 4. Line a baking tray with greaseproof paper.

Whisk the egg whites in a mixing bowl until stiff peaks form. Add the sugar, a tablespoon at a time, whisking well.

Add the chocolate, vinegar and nuts and gently fold into the meringue mixture.

Spoon small mounds of the meringue mixture onto the baking tray. Put in the oven and reduce the temperature to 150°C (130° fan) 300F, gas 2 immediately. Bake for 45-50 minutes. The meringues will be crisp on the outside and chewy in the centre.

Cool on the tray for a few minutes. Place on a wire rack to cool completely.

Raspberry butter cookies

Prep and cook time: 2 hours * makes: 40-50

INGREDIENTS:

400 g | 14 oz | 3 ½ cups plain (all-purpose) flour
125 g | 4 ½ oz | ⅔ cup sugar
1-2 tsp vanilla extract
250 g | 9 oz | 1 cup butter
4 egg yolks

For the topping:
250 g | 9 oz | 1 cup raspberry jam (jelly)
200 g | 7 oz | 1 ½ cups raspberries

METHOD:

Combine all the dough ingredients and quickly knead to a smooth dough. Add a little cold water if the dough is too crumbly. Wrap the dough in cling film and chill for at least an hour.

Heat the oven to 180°C (160°C fan) 375F, gas 5 and line a large baking tray with greaseproof paper.

Divide the dough into 2 portions and form each portion into a roll about 4 cm / 1 ½ " in diameter. Cut the rolls into slices about 1 cm / ½ " thick and flatten slightly. Put them onto the baking tray and bake for 15-20 minutes, until browned.

Place the cookies on a wire rack to cool completely. Push the raspberry jam through a sieve and put a teaspoon of jam on top of each cookie. Add a few raspberries to each cookie.

Chocolate muesli cookies

Prep and cook time: 30 minutes * makes: 25

INGREDIENTS:

150 g | 5 oz | 1 ½ cups mixed nuts
50 g | 2 oz | ½ cup rolled oats
45 g | 1 ½ oz brown sugar
30 ml | 1 fl. oz honey
300 g | 11 oz | 2 cups dark (plain)chocolate,
roughly chopped
150 g | 5 oz | 1 cup milk chocolate,
roughly chopped
1 tbsp groundnut oil

METHOD:

Place the nuts and rolled oats in a food processor
and blend roughly.

Put the sugar and honey in a small pan over a low heat,
allow it to caramelize and then stir in the nut mixture.

Spread the nut mixture out on greaseproof paper,
let it cool and crumble into pieces.

Melt the chocolate with the oil in a bowl over a pan
of simmering water. Let it cool slightly and then drop
spoonfuls onto greaseproof paper.

Leave to set slightly, scatter with the nut mixture
and leave to cool completely.

Cranberry shortbread stars

Prep and cook time: 35 minutes * makes: 15-20

INGREDIENTS:

325 g | 11 oz | 2 ¾ cups plain (all-purpose) flour
200 g | 7 oz | 1 cup unsalted butter
125 g | 4 ½ oz | ½ cup caster (superfine) sugar
2 tsp vanilla extract
2 large egg yolks
110 g | 4 oz | 1 cup dried cranberries

METHOD:

Heat the oven to 180°C (160° fan) 350F, gas 4 and grease a large baking tray with butter.

Sift the flour into a bowl and rub in the butter until the mixture resembles breadcrumbs.

Stir in the remaining ingredients and mix to a dough.

Roll out the dough to a 2 ½ cm / 1 " thickness on a lightly floured surface. Cut into star shapes with a shaped cutter and place on the baking tray.

Bake the stars for 15-20 minutes until pale golden and cooked through. Cool on the baking trays for a few minutes, then place on a wire rack to cool completely.

Chocolate bean cookies

Prep and cook time: 25 minutes * makes: 20

INGREDIENTS:

350 g | 12 oz | 3 cups plain
(all-purpose) flour
1 tsp bicarbonate of soda
(baking soda)
1 tsp baking powder
a pinch of salt
250 g | 9 oz | 1 ⅛ cups butter
300 g | 11 oz | 1 ¼ cups caster
(superfine) sugar
1 egg, beaten
1 tsp vanilla extract
150 g | 5 oz chocolate beans

METHOD:

Heat the oven to 180°C (160° fan) 350F, gas 4 and line 2 baking
trays with greaseproof paper.

Sift the flour, bicarbonate of soda, baking powder and salt into
a mixing bowl, then set aside.

Beat the butter and sugar until fluffy, then beat in the egg
and vanilla. Gradually beat into the sifted dry ingredients
to form a stiff dough.

Roll the dough into 20 balls, then place on the baking trays,
spaced well apart. Press several chocolate beans into each ball
and flatten the balls into disc shapes.

Bake in the oven for 15 minutes until pale golden brown.
Cool on the baking trays for a few minutes, then place
the cookies on a wire rack to cool completely.

Chocolate walnut biscuits

Prep and cook time: 20 minutes * makes: 40

INGREDIENTS:

300 g | 11 oz | 1 ¾ cups chopped
dark (plain) chocolate
110 g | 4 oz | ½ cup butter
3 eggs
250 g | 9 oz | 1 ¼ cups sugar
110 g | 4 oz | 1 cup plain
(all-purpose) flour
1 tsp baking powder
a pinch of salt
2-3 tbsp ground walnuts

To decorate:
150 g | 5 oz chocolate spread
110 g | 4 oz | 1 cup walnuts

METHOD:

Heat the oven to 160°C (140° fan) 325F, gas 3 and line
2 baking trays with greaseproof paper.

Melt the chocolate and butter in a heatproof bowl over a pan
of simmering water and stir until they have melted.

Whisk the eggs and sugar in a clean mixing bowl until creamy.

Sift the flour, baking powder and salt into the egg mixture and
stir until combined. Add the melted chocolate and walnuts.

Place teaspoons of the mixture on the baking trays. Bake the
biscuits for 8 minutes, then cool on the trays for a few minutes.
Place on a wire rack to cool completely.

Spread the chocolate spread on top and place a walnut
on each biscuit.

Lavender biscuits

Prep and cook time: 1 hour 25 minutes * makes: 20

INGREDIENTS:

50 g | 2 oz | ¼ cup grated
white chocolate
150 g | 5 oz | ¾ cup butter, softened
100 g | 3 ½ oz | ½ cup sugar
3 egg yolks
200 g | 7 oz | 1 ¾ cups plain
(all-purpose) flour
100 g | 3 ½ oz | ¾ cup ground almonds
1 tsp baking powder
1 tbsp dried lavender flowers,
finely chopped
demerara sugar

METHOD:

Put all of the ingredients, except the demerara sugar, in a
mixing bowl and knead into a smooth dough. If the dough
is too crumbly add 1-2 tablespoons water.

Shape the dough into a 3 cm / 1 ½ " thick roll. Roll the dough
in the demerara sugar, then wrap in cling film and chill for at
least 1 hour.

Heat the oven to 180°C (160° fan) 350F, gas 4 and line a large
baking tray with greaseproof paper.

Cut 1 cm thick slices from the roll and press the surface of
each biscuit in demerara sugar.

Place on the baking tray and bake for 15 minutes until golden.
Cool on the baking tray for a few minutes, then place on a wire
rack to cool completely.

Vanilla moon biscuits

Prep and cook time: 50 minutes * makes: 30-40

INGREDIENTS:

2 vanilla pods
100 g | 3 ½ oz | ½ cup sugar
200 g | 7 oz | 1 cup butter
250 g | 9 oz | 2 ½ cups plain
(all-purpose) flour
1 egg yolk
100 g | 3 ½ oz | ¾ cup ground almonds
60 g | 2 oz icing (confectioners') sugar

METHOD:

Split the vanilla pods lengthwise and scrape out the seeds.
Mix with the sugar and set aside.

Beat the butter in a mixing bowl until soft. Beat in the egg yolk,
ground almonds and 70 g of the vanilla sugar to form a dough.
Shape it into a ball, wrap in cling film and chill for at least
30 minutes.

Heat the oven to 190°C (170° fan) 375F, gas 5. Line a large
baking tray with greaseproof paper.

Divide the dough into rolls, each about 3 cm / 1 " in diameter.
Curve the rolls into crescents and put them on the baking tray.

Bake for 10-15 minutes until lightly golden and cooked through.
Cool slightly on the tray.

Mix the remaining vanilla sugar with the icing sugar and roll
the warm biscuits in the mixture.

Plum and almond cookies

Prep and cook time: 25 minutes * makes: 40

INGREDIENTS:

4 eggs
250 g | 9 oz | 1 ¼ cups sugar
125 g | 4 ½ oz | ¾ cup ground almonds
120 g | 4 oz | ¾ cup dried prunes,
finely chopped
½ tsp ground cinnamon
a pinch of ground cloves
1 tsp bicarbonate of soda
(baking soda)
500 g | 18 oz | 4 ½ cups plain
(all-purpose) flour

METHOD:

Heat the oven to 180°C (160° fan) 350F, gas 4. Line 2 baking trays with greaseproof paper.

Beat the eggs with the sugar until fluffy. Fold in the almonds and prunes.

Sift in the cinnamon, cloves, bicarbonate of soda and the flour and mix to a dough.

Roll small pieces of the dough with floured hands into balls. Place on the baking trays and flatten with a fork.

Bake for 15-18 minutes, until golden. Cool on the trays for a few minutes, then place them on a wire rack to cool completely.

Florentines

Prep and cook time: 25 minutes * makes: 20

INGREDIENTS:

140 g | ¾ cup | 5 oz light brown sugar

100 ml | 3 ½ fl. oz clear honey

200 g | 7 oz | 1 cup butter

100 g | 3 ½ oz desiccated (flaked) coconut

140 g | 5 oz | 2 cups flaked (slivered) almonds

200 g | 7 oz | 1 cup glace (candied) cherries, quartered

100 g | 3 ½ oz | 1 ⅓ cups candied peel, diced

60 g | 1 oz plain (all-purpose) flour

250 g | 9 oz | 1 ½ cups dark (plain) chocolate, chopped

METHOD:

Heat the oven to 200°C (180° fan) 400F, gas 6. Line 2 large baking trays with greaseproof paper.

Put the sugar, honey and butter in a large pan and heat until melted.

Stir in the coconut, almonds, cherries, reserve some for the decoration, peel and flour until blended.

Place balls of the mixture on the tray, and flatten thinly. Bake for 10-12 minutes until golden. Leave to cool and firm up a little, but not set hard.

Melt the chocolate in a heatproof bowl over a pan of simmering water.

Turn the florentines out onto the 2nd lined tray and peel off the baking paper. Spread the melted chocolate over one side.

Place a glace cherry in the centre of each florentine.

Pumpkin cookies

Prep and cook time: 25 minutes * makes: 30

INGREDIENTS:

225 g | 8 oz | 1 cup butter
200 g | 7 oz | 1 cup caster
(superfine) sugar
175 g | 6 oz | 1 cup dark brown sugar
1 egg
1 tsp vanilla extract
250 g | 9 oz | 1 cup pumpkin puree
80 g | 3 oz | 1 cup rolled oats
1 tsp baking powder
1 tsp ground cinnamon
½ tsp salt
150 g | 5 oz | 1 cup raisins
300 g | 11 oz | 2 ¾ cups plain
(all-purpose) flour

METHOD:

Heat the oven to 180°C (160° fan) 350F, gas 4. Line 2 baking trays with greaseproof paper.

Beat the butter and sugars in a mixing bowl until fluffy. Beat in the egg, vanilla and pumpkin. Stir in the remaining ingredients until they form a smooth batter.

Drop heaped teaspoons on to the baking trays and bake for 12-15 minutes, until slightly browned.

Cool the cookies on the baking trays for a few minutes, then place them on a wire rack to cool completely.

Chocolate star biscuits

Prep and cook time: 1 hour 25 minutes * makes: 30

INGREDIENTS:

180 g | 6 oz | 1 ½ cups plain
(all-purpose) flour
40 g | 1 ½ oz | ⅓ cup cocoa
½ tsp ground cinnamon
a pinch of ground cloves
a pinch of ground allspice
125 g | 4 ½ oz | ½ cup butter
50 g | 2 oz | ¼ cup brown sugar
75 g | 2 ½ oz | ½ cup ground almonds
1 egg, beaten
1 tbsp espresso, cooled
½ tsp vanilla extract

METHOD:

Sift the flour, cocoa and spices into a mixing bowl.
Rub in the butter until the mixture resembles breadcrumbs.
Stir in the sugar and ground almonds.

Add the egg, coffee and vanilla and mix the ingredients
to form a dough. Wrap in cling film and chill for 1 hour.

Heat the oven to 180°C (160° fan) 350F, gas 4 and line
a baking tray with greaseproof paper.

Roll out the dough between sheets of greaseproof paper,
1 cm / ½ " thick, and cut out stars with a shaped cutter.

Bake for 10-12 minutes until firm and then sprinkle with
sugar while warm. Cool on the baking trays for a few minutes,
then place the biscuits on a wire rack to cool completely.

Hazelnut chewies

Prep and cook time: 25 minutes * makes: 40

INGREDIENTS:

200 g | 7 oz | 1 cup butter
200 g | 7 oz | 1 cup sugar
3 eggs
250 g | 9 oz | 2 ½ cups plain
(all-purpose) flour
150 g | 5 oz | 1 cup ground
hazelnuts (cobnuts)
2 tsp baking powder
45 g | 1 ½ oz cocoa powder
½ tsp ground cinnamon
120 ml | 4 fl. oz | ½ cup milk
50 g | 2 oz | ½ cup icing
(confectioners') sugar
1 tsp lemon juice
50 g | 2 oz | ⅓ cup chopped hazelnuts

METHOD:

Heat the oven to 160°C (140° fan) 325F, gas 3 and line
2 baking trays with greaseproof paper.

Beat the butter and sugar in a mixing bowl until light and fluffy.

Beat each egg in separately. In a separate bowl, mix the flour,
hazelnuts, baking powder, cocoa powder and cinnamon together,
then mix into the egg mixture, alternating with the milk.

Beat the icing sugar with the lemon juice and enough water
to give a thin coating consistency.

Put tablespoons of the mixture on the baking trays, spread
thinly with the lemon coating and sprinkle with the hazelnuts.

Bake the chewies for 10-12 minutes. Cool them on the
baking trays for a few minutes, then place on a wire rack
to cool completely.

Lemon cream biscuits

Prep and cook time: 35 minutes * makes: 10

INGREDIENTS:

225 g | 8 oz | 1 cup unsalted butter
110 g | 4 oz | ¾ cup icing
(confectioners') sugar
1 lemon, zest
375 g | 13 oz | 3 cups plain
(all-purpose) flour
a pinch of salt

For the lemon cream:
75 g | 2 ½ oz | ⅓ cup butter
110 g | 4 oz | 1 cup icing sugar
2 tsp lemon juice
1 lemon, zest

METHOD:

Heat the oven to 180°C (160° fan) 350F, gas 4 and line
2 baking trays with greaseproof paper.

Beat the butter and icing sugar together in a large bowl until
combined and stir in the lemon zest.

Sift in the flour and salt and work the mixture together to
form a stiff dough, then knead lightly for a few moments
until smooth, but avoid over handling.

Roll out the dough to a thickness of about 5 mm / ¼ " and
use a medium, smooth-edged cutter to cut out 20 biscuits.

Place the biscuits on to the baking trays, evenly spaced.
Bake for 12-15 minutes until pale golden brown. Cool the
biscuits on the trays for 5 minutes, then place them on a wire
rack to cool completely.

For the lemon cream, cream the butter until soft, then sift in
the icing sugar and beat well. Stir in the lemon juice and zest.

Sandwich the cooled biscuits together with the lemon cream.

Heart-shaped jam biscuits

Prep and cook time: 1 hour 20 minutes * makes: 16

INGREDIENTS:

150 g | 5 oz | ¾ cup butter
75 g | 2 ½ oz | ⅓ cup caster
(superfine) sugar
100 g | 3 ½ oz | 1 cup plain
(all-purpose) flour
1 egg, beaten
75 g | 2 ½ oz seedless strawberry
jam (jelly)

METHOD:

Heat the oven to 160°C (140° fan) 325F, gas 3. Grease a large baking tray with butter.

Beat the butter until soft and fluffy then beat in the sugar and then the flour. Knead gently to form a stiff dough and chill for 30 minutes. Roll onto a floured board to a thickness of about ½ cm / ¼ ". Using a large, heart-shaped cutter, cut an even number of shapes from the dough.

Using a smaller heart-shaped cutter, cut the middles out of half the large heart shapes. Put the large heart shapes without the middles cut away, onto the baking tray and moisten them with a little water. Lay the large shapes with the middles cut away on top of the shapes on the tray and gently press the two together.

Brush the tops of the biscuits with the beaten egg. Put a teaspoon of the jam in the middle of each biscuit and bake for 20-30 minutes, until the biscuits are golden brown.

Cool on the baking tray for a few minutes, then place on a wire rack to cool completely.

Coconut biscuits

Prep and cook time: 25 minutes * makes: 15

INGREDIENTS:

60 g | 2 oz butter
125 g | 4 ½ oz caster (superfine) sugar
1 egg, beaten
150 g | 5 oz | 1 ¼ cups plain
(all-purpose) flour
75 g | 2 ½ oz | 1 cup desiccated (flaked)
coconut

To decorate:
granulated sugar

METHOD:

Heat the oven to 180°C (160° fan) 350F, gas 4. Line a large baking tray with greaseproof paper.

Beat the butter and sugar in a mixing bowl until smooth. Beat in the egg, flour and coconut to form a dough.

Roll pieces of the dough into small balls and place apart, on the baking tray.

Bake for 15-20 minutes until golden. Sprinkle with sugar.

Cool on the baking tray for a few minutes, then place on a wire rack to cool completely.

Sprinkle star cookies

Prep and cook time: 40 minutes * makes: 24

INGREDIENTS:

110 g | 4 oz | ½ cup unsalted butter
110 g | 4 oz | ¾ cup dark brown sugar
300 g | 11 oz | 2 ½ cups plain
(all-purpose) flour
a pinch of salt
1 tsp baking powder
1 tsp ground cinnamon
¼ tsp ground cloves
½ tsp mixed spice
2 large eggs, beaten
60 ml | 2 fl. oz clear honey

To decorate:
300 g | 11 oz icing
(confectioners') sugar
45 ml | 1 ½ fl. oz water
coloured sugar sprinkles

METHOD:

For the biscuits, heat the oven to 160°C (140° fan) 325F, gas 3.
Line 2 baking trays with greaseproof paper.

Beat the butter and sugar in a mixing bowl until smooth
and creamy. Sift in the flour, salt, baking powder, cinnamon,
cloves and mixed spice and stir until smooth.

Beat in the eggs and honey to form a dough. If the dough
is too dry add a little water, if it is too wet, add a little flour.

Roll out the dough on a lightly floured surface, about
5 mm / ¼ " thick. Cut star shapes out of the dough using
a shaped cutter.

Place the biscuits on the baking trays and bake for 20 minutes
until golden brown and cooked through. Place on a wire rack
to cool completely.

To decorate, prepare the icing according to the pack instructions.
Ice the edges of the biscuits using a teaspoon, using a small
piping bag. Put a little icing in the centre of each biscuit and
sprinkle with the sugar sprinkles.

Nougat chocolate biscuits

Prep and cook time: 25 minutes * makes: 20

INGREDIENTS:

175 g | 6 oz | ¾ cup butter
75 g | 2 ½ oz | ½ cup icing
(confectioners') sugar
¼ tsp salt
1 tsp vanilla extract
1 egg white
200 g | 7 oz | 1 ¾ cups plain
(all-purpose) flour
25 g | 1 oz | ¼ cup cornflour (cornstarch)
150 g | 5 oz chocolate nougat
150 g | 5 oz | ¾ cup dark (plain)
chocolate, chopped

METHOD:

Heat the oven to 200°C (180° fan) 400F, gas 6. Line a baking tray with greaseproof paper.

Beat the butter with the sugar, salt and vanilla in a mixing bowl. Add the egg white and stir until blended.

Sift in the flour and cornflour and stir well. Put the mixture into a piping bag with a star nozzle about 10 mm diameter. Pipe rounds onto the baking tray.

Bake for oven 8-12 minutes, until golden. Cool on the baking trays for a few minutes, then place on a wire rack to cool completely.

Melt the nougat in a heatproof bowl over a pan of simmering water. Spread half of the biscuits with the nougat and place another biscuit on top.

Melt the chocolate and dip the biscuits in the chocolate. Place on greaseproof paper and leave to set.

Heart-shaped thins

Prep and cook time: 1 hour 25 minutes * makes: 40

INGREDIENTS:

250 g | 9 oz | 2 ½ cups plain
(all-purpose) flour
125 g | 4 ½ oz | 1 ¼ cups icing
(confectioners') sugar
1 lemon, zest
1 egg
150 g | 5 oz | ¾ cup butter, diced

To decorate:
125 g | 4 ½ oz | 1 ¼ cups icing sugar
1 tbsp raspberry syrup
1-2 tbsp lemon juice
edible silver baubles

METHOD:

Mix the flour, icing sugar and lemon zest in a mixing bowl.
Beat in the egg and butter and knead with your hands into a
firm dough. Wrap the dough in cling film and chill for 1 hour.

Heat the oven to 180°C (160° fan) 350F, gas 4 and line a
large baking tray with greaseproof paper.

Roll out the dough on a floured surface, 2-3 mm thick.
Cut out heart shapes using a shaped cutter and place
on the baking tray.

Bake for about 10 minutes until golden brown. Cool the
biscuits on the baking trays for a few minutes, then place
on a wire rack to cool completely.

To decorate, sift the icing sugar into a bowl and stir in the
raspberry syrup and lemon juice until thick and smooth.

Spoon the icing into a piping bag and pipe onto the biscuits.
Press the silver baubles into the icing and leave to set.

Macadamia biscuits

Prep and cook time: 1 hour 25 minutes * makes: 30

INGREDIENTS:

175 g | 6 oz | ¾ cup butter
100 g | 3 ½ oz | ½ cup sugar
a pinch of salt
1 vanilla pod, insides scraped out
1 tsp ground cinnamon
200 g | 7 oz | 1 ¾ cups plain
(all-purpose) flour
1 tsp baking powder
150 g | 5 oz | 1 ⅛ cups chopped
macadamia nuts
1 egg

To decorate:
macadamia nuts, finely chopped

METHOD:

Beat the butter, sugar and salt in a mixing bowl until fluffy.

Stir in the vanilla and cinnamon, followed by the flour,
baking powder and nuts. Beat in the egg to form a smooth
dough. Shape into a ball and wrap in cling film. Chill for 1 hour.

Heat the oven to 180°C (160° fan) 350F, gas 4. Line 2 baking
trays with greaseproof paper.

Roll into small balls with wet hands and place about
3 cm / 1" apart on the baking trays.

Bake for 10-15 minutes until golden. Sprinkle with the
chopped nuts. Cool on the baking tray for a few minutes,
then place on a wire rack to cool completely.

Lime curd shortbreads

Prep and cook time: 55 minutes ∗ makes: 12

INGREDIENTS:

125 g | 4 ½ oz | ½ cup unsalted butter
50 g | 2 oz | ¼ cup caster
(superfine) sugar
180 g | 6 oz | 1 ½ cups plain
(all-purpose) flour
150 g | 5 oz | ½ cup lime curd

To decorate:
icing (confectioners') sugar

METHOD:

Beat the butter and sugar in a mixing bowl until smooth and stir
in the flour to form a dough.

Roll the dough out on a floured surface to a 1 cm / ½ " thickness.
Cut into rounds and place on a baking tray greased with butter.
Chill the shortbread rounds for 20 minutes.

Heat the oven to 190°C (170° fan) 375F, gas 5.

Bake the shortbread biscuits for 15-20 minutes, until slightly
golden. Cool on the baking trays for a few minutes, then place
on a wire rack to cool completely.

Sandwich the biscuits together with lime curd and sift
a little icing sugar over the top.

MACAROONS.

Making macaroons

Prep and cook time: 1 hour 45 minutes * makes: 30

INGREDIENTS:

4 tbsp plain (all-purpose) flour
200 g | 7 oz | 1 cup ground almonds
2 tsp cocoa powder
4 egg whites
250 g | 9 oz | 1 cups caster
(superfine) sugar

For the filling:
150 g | 5 oz | ¾ cup dark
chocolate, chopped
80 ml | 3 fl oz | ⅓ cup double cream
20 g | ¾ oz butter
cocoa powder

METHOD:

Macaroons are a delicacy but they do not have to be difficult to make. Look at the simple step-by-step pictures on the opposite page and follow the instructions to master the techniques.

Heat the oven to 140°C (120° fan) 275F, gas 1. Line a large baking tray with greaseproof paper.

Mix the flour with the almonds and cocoa in a bowl.

Whisk the egg whites until stiff. Gradually whisk in the sugar until shiny.

Gently stir in the almond mixture until combined.

Spoon the mixture into a piping bag and pipe rounds onto the baking tray, about 3 cm / 1 " in diameter.

Bake for about 45 minutes, until firm and risen. Cool on the baking tray for a few minutes, then place on a wire rack to cool completely.

For the filling, heat the chocolate, cream and butter in a small pan until the chocolate and butter have melted. Stir and set aside to cool, then chill until thick.

Sandwich the macaroons with the filling. Decorate the macaroons as desired.

Macaroons with pistachio cream

Prep and cook time: 25 minutes ∗ makes: 8

INGREDIENTS:

220 g | 8 oz | 1 ½ cups
ground almonds
175 g | 6 oz | ¾ cup caster sugar
2 egg whites, lightly beaten

For the pistachio cream:
300 ml | 11 fl. oz | 1 ⅓ cups
double cream
75 g | 2 ½ oz | ¾ cup unsalted
pistachios, chopped
icing (confectioners') sugar

METHOD:

Heat the oven to 180°C (160° fan) 350F, gas 4. Line a large baking tray with greaseproof paper.

Put the ground almonds in a bowl with the sugar and egg whites. Stir to combine until firm, yet slightly sticky.

Roll heaped teaspoonfuls of the mixture into balls and place on the baking tray. Flatten slightly with a wet fork.

Bake for about 10 minutes, until golden. Cool on the baking trays for a few minutes, then place on a wire rack to cool completely.

For the pistachio cream, whisk the cream until it forms soft peaks. Gently fold in the pistachios and sweeten to taste with icing sugar.

Sandwich the macaroons together with the pistachio cream.

Valentines macaroons

Prep and cook time: 1 hour * Makes: makes: 30

INGREDIENTS:

4 egg whites
2 tsp lemon juice
250 g | 9 oz | 1 ¼ cups caster
(superfine) sugar
200 g | 7 oz | 2 cups ground almonds
2 tsp cocoa powder

For the filling:
150 g | 5 oz | ¾ cup chopped dark
(plain) chocolate
80 ml | 3 fl. oz | ⅓ cup cream
20 g | ½ oz butter, chopped
cocoa powder, to dust

METHOD:

Heat the oven to 130°C (110° fan) 270F, gas 1 and line a large baking tray with greaseproof paper.

Whisk the egg whites with the lemon juice until they form stiff peaks, then gradually add the sugar while whisking. Continue whisking until the mixture is firm and glossy.

Carefully fold in the ground almonds and cocoa. Spoon the mixture into a piping bag with a large, round nozzle and pipe small domed circles approximately 4 mm / ¾ " in diameter onto the baking tray.

Bake for about 40 minutes, leaving the oven door open a little. Cool on the baking trays for a few minutes, then place the macaroons on a wire rack to cool completely.

To make the filling, melt the chocolate in a heatproof bowl over a pan of simmering water.

Whisk the cream until thick. Whisk the butter into the melted chocolate and leave to cool.

Fold in the cream and then sandwich the macaroons together with the chocolate cream.

Put a heart-shaped stencil on top of each macaroon, dust with cocoa and carefully remove the stencil.

Almond macaroons

Prep and cook time: 1 hour 5 minutes * makes: 32

INGREDIENTS:

1 large egg
150 g | 5 oz | 1 ½ cups icing
(confectioners') sugar
250 g | 9 oz | 1 ½ cups ground almonds
2 tsp grated lemon zest
½ tsp almond extract

METHOD:

Heat the oven to 160°C (140° fan) 325F, gas 3 and line
2 large baking trays with greaseproof paper.

Whisk the egg with the icing sugar for about 7 minutes,
until very creamy. Gradually add the almonds, lemon zest
and almond extract to form a soft paste.

Knead briefly to form a smooth dough. Wrap the dough in cling
film and let it rest for 30 minutes at room temperature. Shape it
into a roll and divide it into 32 pieces.

Form the pieces into balls and place apart on the baking trays,
flattening slightly.

Bake for about 20 minutes, until golden. Cool on the
baking trays for a few minutes, then place on a wire
rack to cool completely.

Macaroons with caramel butter

Prep and cook time: 45 minutes * makes: 10

INGREDIENTS:

110 g | 4 oz | ½ cup caster
(superfine) sugar
175 g | 6 oz | 1 cup ground almonds
1 egg white, beaten
1 tsp almond extract

For the caramel butter:
110 g | 4 oz | ½ cup butter
200 g | 7 oz | 1 cup brown sugar
50 ml | 2 fl. oz milk
1 tsp vanilla extract
400 g | 14 oz | 4 cups icing
(confectioners') sugar

METHOD:

Heat the oven to 160°C (140° fan) 325F, gas 3. Line a large baking tray with greaseproof paper.

Combine the sugar and ground almonds, mixing them very well so that the oil from the almonds is absorbed by the sugar.

Stir in the egg white and almond extract until the mixture forms a firm paste. Dampen your hands and form the mixture into small balls.

Space the balls 3 cm / 1 " apart on the baking tray. Bake for 20-25 minutes until firm and lightly coloured. Cool on the baking tray for a few minutes, then place on a wire rack to cool completely.

For the caramel butter, melt the butter and sugar in a pan. Increase the heat to boiling point, stirring frequently. Boil and stir for 1 minute until thickened. Remove from the heat and add the milk. Whisk until smooth. Add the vanilla and whisk again.

Sift in enough icing sugar until it's a spreading consistency. Stand for 5 minutes, stirring occasionally, until thickened.

Sandwich the macaroons together with the caramel butter.

Amaretti macaroons

Prep and cook time: 35 minutes * makes: 30

INGREDIENTS:

3 egg whites
300 g | 11 oz | 2 cups ground almonds
1 tbsp Amaretto
300 g | 11 oz | 1 ¾ cups sugar
50 g | 2 oz | ¼ cup coarse
sugar crystals

METHOD:

Heat the oven to 160°C (140° fan) 325F, gas 3. Line a large baking tray with greaseproof paper.

Whisk the egg whites until stiff. Whisk in the almonds, amaretto and sugar until shiny.

Shape the mixture into walnut-sized balls and place apart on the baking tray. Flatten slightly.

Bake for 20-25 minutes until firm and golden. Sprinkle with coarse sugar while warm. Cool on the baking trays for a few minutes, then place on a wire rack to cool completely.

Chocolate-dipped coconut macaroons

Prep and cook time: 30 minutes * makes: 15-20

INGREDIENTS:

2 egg whites

2 tsp cornflour (cornstarch)

115 g | 4 oz | ½ cup caster (superfine) sugar

115 g | 4 oz | 1 ¼ cups desiccated (shredded) coconut

110 g | 4 oz | ¾ cup dark (plain) chocolate, chopped

METHOD:

Heat the oven to 180°C (160° fan) 350F, gas 4. Line a baking tray with greaseproof paper.

Whisk the egg whites until frothy, but not stiff. Stir in the cornflour and sugar, followed by the coconut.

Drop the mixture in heaps on the baking tray. Bake for about 20 minutes until firm and golden brown. Cool on the baking tray for a few minutes, then place on a wire rack to cool completely.

Melt the chocolate in a heatproof bowl over a pan of simmering water. Dip the base of each macaroon in the chocolate and place on greaseproof paper to set.

Chocolate and fig macaroons

Prep and cook time: 50 minutes * makes: 25-30

INGREDIENTS:

3 egg whites
1 tsp lemon juice
a pinch of salt
200 g | 7 oz | 1 cup sugar
200 g | 7 oz | 2 cups ground almonds
30 g | 1 oz cornflour (cornstarch)
30 g | 1 oz cocoa powder
½ tsp ground cinnamon

For the filling:
200 g | 7 oz | 1 ¼ cups dried figs
1-2 tbsp almond liqueur
100 g | 3 ½ oz marzipan, finely grated

METHOD:

Heat the oven to 180°C (160° fan) 350F, gas 4. Line a large baking tray with greaseproof paper.

Whisk the egg whites with the lemon juice, salt and sugar until the sugar has dissolved and the egg whites are glossy and form very stiff peaks.

Mix the almonds, cornflour, cocoa powder and cinnamon together and fold them carefully into the egg whites.

Spoon the mixture into a piping bag with a large nozzle and pipe around 50-60 small, evenly spaced mounds, onto the baking tray. Bake the macaroons for 25-30 minutes until firm and golden. Place them on a wire rack to cool completely.

For the filling, place the figs and liqueur in a food processor and blend to a puree. Scrape the figs into a bowl with the grated marzipan and mix well.

Divide the fig marzipan into 25-30 pieces, roll them into balls and flatten slightly. Place a piece of fig marzipan between two macaroons and gently press together.

Pink macaroons

Prep and cook time: 50 minutes * makes: 20

INGREDIENTS:

4 egg whites
300 g | 11 oz | 3 cups icing
(confectioners') sugar
pink food dye
140 g | 5 oz | 1 cup ground almonds
150 ml | 5 fl. oz | ⅔ cup double cream

METHOD:

Heat the oven to 180°C (160° fan) 350F, gas 4. Line 2 large
baking trays with greaseproof paper.

Whisk the egg whites in a large bowl until soft peaks form.
Gradually whisk in the icing sugar.

Add a few drops of dye with the final addition of sugar.
Keep whisking until the mixture is light pink, thick and glossy.

Gently fold in the ground almonds.

Spoon 40 rounds onto the baking trays, each about 5 cm /
2 " wide. Leave to stand for 10 minutes until a skin starts to form.

Place the baking trays in the oven, leaving the oven door slightly
ajar to allow steam to escape, then bake for 20-25 minutes until
just crisp, but not browned. Leave to cool.

Whisk the cream until stiff and sandwich the macaroons together.

Luxemburgerli macaroons

Prep and cook time: 50 minutes * makes: 20

INGREDIENTS:

175 g | 6 oz | 1 ¼ cups icing (confectioners') sugar
125 g | 4 ½ oz | 1 cup ground almonds
3 egg whites
75 g | 2 ½ oz caster (superfine) sugar
½ tsp raspberry extract
pink food dye
½ tsp cocoa powder
1 tsp strong espresso

For the fillings:
150 g | 5 oz | ¾ cup butter
75 g | 2 ½ oz | ¾ cup icing (confectioners') sugar
pink food dye
½ tsp instant espresso powder
½ tsp cocoa powder

METHOD:

Blend the icing sugar and ground almonds in a food processor until very fine.

Whisk the egg whites to soft peaks, then gradually whisk in the caster sugar until thick and glossy. Fold in the almond and icing sugar mixture until combined.

Divide the mixture into 3 bowls. Add the raspberry extract and pink dye to 1 bowl, cocoa to another and espresso to the 3rd bowl.

Spoon 40 small rounds onto a baking tray lined with greaseproof paper. Leave to stand for 10-15 minutes to form a slight skin.

Heat the oven to 160°C (140° fan) 325F, gas 3.

Bake for 15 minutes until firm. Cool on the baking trays for a few minutes, then place on a wire rack to cool completely.

For the fillings, beat the butter until creamy, then sift in the icing sugar and beat until smooth.

Divide into 3 bowls and add pink dye, espresso powder and cocoa powder to each bowl. Beat until smooth.

Sandwich the macaroons together with the buttercream.

Vanilla macaroons

Prep and cook time: 50 minutes * makes: 10-12

INGREDIENTS:

225 g | 8 oz | 1 cup caster
(superfine) sugar
110 g | 4 oz | ¾ cup ground almonds
25 g | 1 oz | ¼ cup rice flour
2 egg whites, beaten
few drops vanilla extract

For the vanilla buttercream:
110 g | 4 oz | ½ cup butter
200 g | 7 oz | 2 cups icing
(confectioners') sugar
1 vanilla pod (bean)

METHOD:

Heat the oven to 160°C (140° fan) 325F, gas 3.
Line a large baking tray with greaseproof paper.

Combine the sugar, ground almonds and rice flour,
then stir in the egg whites and vanilla.

Place 20-24 spoonfuls of the mixture onto the baking tray.
Bake for 20-25 minutes until firm. Cool on the baking tray
for a few minutes, then place on a wire rack to cool completely.

For the vanilla buttercream, beat the butter until soft
and sift in the icing sugar.

Split the vanilla pod lengthwise and scrape the seeds
into the buttercream and beat well.

Sandwich the macaroons together with the buttercream.

Macarons à la violette de Toulouse

Prep and cook time: 45 minutes * makes: 10

INGREDIENTS:

3 egg whites
30 g | 1 oz | ⅛ cup sugar
200 g | 7 oz | 2 cups icing
(confectioners') sugar
110 g | 4 oz | ¾ cup ground almonds
2 tbsp crystallised violet petals, crushed

For the filling:
110 g | 4 oz | ½ cup sugar
2 large egg whites
175 g | 6 oz | ¾ cup unsalted butter
30 ml | 1 fl. oz violet liqueur
violet food dye (optional)

To decorate:
2 tbsp crystallised violet petals, crushed
sliced strawberries
icing sugar

METHOD:

Whisk the egg whites to a foam, gradually adding the sugar
until you obtain a glossy meringue.

Grind the almonds and icing sugar in a food processor
and fold into the meringue with the crushed violet petals.

Spoon large rounds onto a baking tray lined with greaseproof
paper and leave to stand for 30 minutes to dry out.

Heat the oven to 150°C (130° fan) 300F, gas 2.

Bake for 15-20 minutes, depending on size. Cool on the
baking tray for a few minutes, then place on a wire rack
to cool completely.

For the filling, put the sugar and egg whites in a large heatproof
bowl over a pan of simmering water and whisk constantly,
keeping the mixture over the heat, until it feels hot to the touch.
Remove from the heat and whisk to a thick, shiny meringue.

Gradually beat in the butter and whisk until thick and smooth.
Beat in the liqueur food dye.

Sandwich the macaroons together with the violet cream. Place
a few sliced strawberries on top of each macaroon and sprinkle
with crushed violet petals. Sift over a little icing sugar.

Lemon almond macaroons

Prep and cook time: 1 hour * makes: 15

INGREDIENTS:

4 egg whites
1 lemon, juice and zest
250 g | 9 oz | 1 ⅛ cups caster
(superfine) sugar
200 g | 7 oz | 1 ⅓ cups ground almonds

For the filling:
100 g | 3 ½ oz | ¾ cup dark (plain)
chocolate, chopped
30 ml | 1 fl. oz cream
1 tbsp butter
1 tbsp kirsch

METHOD:

Heat the oven to 150°C (130° fan) 300F, gas 2 and line a large baking tray with greaseproof paper.

Whisk the egg whites and a tablespoon of lemon juice until stiff. Gradually whisk in the sugar and lemon zest until incorporated.

Continue whisking until shiny, then fold in the almonds. Spoon or pipe the mixture into rounds on the baking tray and bake for about 40 minutes, leaving the oven door ajar slightly. Cool on the baking tray for a few minutes, then place the macaroons on a wire rack to cool completely.

For the cream filling, melt the chocolate in a heatproof bowl over a pan of simmering water. Whisk in the cream and butter, then stir in the kirsch. Leave the cream to cool until thickened, the use the chocolate cream to sandwich the macaroons together.

Macaroons with chocolate cream

Prep and cook time: 50 minutes * makes: 12

INGREDIENTS:

150 g | 5 oz | 1 ½ cups icing (confectioners') sugar
100 g | 3 ½ oz | ¾ cup ground almonds
2 egg whites
100 g | 3 ½ oz | ¾ cup milk or dark (plain) chocolate, chopped
2 tsp cream

METHOD:

Heat the oven to 180°C (160° fan) 350F, gas 4 and line a large baking tray with greaseproof paper.

Sift the icing sugar into a mixing bowl and stir in the ground almonds. In a separate bowl, whisk the egg whites until stiff then fold them into the dry ingredients.

Spoon or pipe 24 evenly spaced rounds about 3 cm / 1 " in diameter onto the baking tray. Leave to stand for 15 minutes to dry out.

Bake for 15-20 minutes until firm. Cool the macaroons on the baking tray for a few minutes, then place on a wire rack to cool completely.

For the filling, melt half of the chocolate in a heatproof bowl over a pan of simmering water and stir in the cream until smooth. Leave the filling to cool and thicken a little, then sandwich the macaroons together using a teaspoon of chocolate cream.

Melt the remaining chocolate as before and drizzle over the top of the macaroons.

Pistachio macaroons

Prep and cook time: 25 minutes * makes: 15

INGREDIENTS:

140 g | 5 oz | 1 ¼ cups unsalted
pistachios, chopped
250 g | 9 oz | 2 ¼ cups icing
(confectioners') sugar
2 egg whites

For the pistachio cream:
300 ml | 11 fl. oz | 1 ⅓ cups
double cream
75 g | 2 ½ oz | ¾ cup unsalted pistachios,
chopped
icing (confectioners') sugar

METHOD:

Grind the pistachios and 25 g of icing sugar in a food
processor until fine. Mix with 175 g icing sugar in a large bowl.

Whisk the egg whites until stiff, add the remaining icing sugar
and whisk again until thick and glossy. Fold into the nut mixture.

Spoon, or pipe, 30 small blobs of the mixture well apart on a
baking tray lined with greaseproof paper. Leave to stand for
30 minutes, to dry.

Meanwhile, heat the oven to 160°C (140° fan) 325F, gas 3.

Bake for 12-15 minutes until firm. Cool on the baking trays for
a few minutes, then place on a wire rack to cool completely.

For the pistachio cream, whisk the cream until it forms soft
peaks. Gently fold in the pistachios and sweeten to taste
with icing sugar.

Sandwich the macaroons together with the pistachio cream.

Mascarpone and macaroon tartlet with berries

Prep and cook time: 45 minutes * makes: 12

INGREDIENTS:

3 egg whites
300 g | 11 oz | 2 cups ground almonds
300 g | 11 oz | 2 cups sugar

For the filling and decoration:
200 g | 7 oz | 1 cup mascarpone
30 ml | 1 fl. oz raspberry liqueur
60 ml | 2 fl. oz agave syrup
300 g | 11 oz | 2 ⅓ cups mixed berries
1 tbsp icing (confectioners') sugar

METHOD:

Heat the oven to 160°C (140° fan) 325F, gas 3. Line a large baking tray with greaseproof paper. Whisk the egg whites until stiff.

Mix the almonds with the sugar and fold into the egg whites.

Shape the mixture into walnut-sized balls, flatten slightly and place apart on the baking tray.

Bake for about 25 minutes until firm. Cool on the baking trays for a few minutes, then place on a wire rack to cool completely.

Mix the mascarpone with the raspberry liqueur and agave syrup. Sift a little icing sugar over the berries.

Sandwich 3 macaroons with the mascarpone mixture and decorate with the berries.

Almond macaroons

Prep and cook time: 25 minutes * makes: 9

INGREDIENTS:

2 egg whites
1 tsp almond extract
140 g | 5 oz | 1 cup ground almonds
110 g | 4 ½ oz | ¾ cup light
brown sugar

METHOD:

Heat the oven to 180°C (160° fan) 350F, gas 4. Line a large baking tray with greaseproof paper.

Whisk the egg whites until stiff. Whisk in the almond extract.

Gently stir in the ground almonds and sugar until combined.

Place 9 small spoonfuls on the baking tray, well apart and flatten slightly.

Bake for 15 minutes, until risen and golden. Cool on the baking tray for a few minutes, then place on a wire rack to cool completely.

Chocolate amaretti macaroons

Prep and cook time: 25 minutes * makes: 20

INGREDIENTS:

For the chocolate cream:
150 g | 5 oz | ¾ cup dark (plain) chocolate, chopped
75 ml | 2 ½ fl. oz | ⅓ cup double cream

For the amaretti:
200 g | 7 oz | 1 ¼ cups ground almonds
100 g | 3 ½ oz | ½ cup sugar
2 drops bitter almond oil
2 egg whites
40 g | 1 ½ oz | ½ cup icing (confectioners') sugar

METHOD:

For the chocolate cream, melt the chocolate with the cream in a small pan. Cool overnight in the refrigerator.

For the amaretti, heat the oven to 160°C (140° fan) 325F, gas 3. Line a large baking tray with greaseproof paper.

Mix the almonds, 50 g sugar and bitter almond oil together.

Whisk the egg whites with the remaining sugar until stiff and shiny. Gently stir in the almond mixture.

Spoon or pipe 40 small circles on the baking tray. Sift over the icing sugar and bake for 10-15 minutes until golden. Turn off the oven and leave the macaroons in the oven to dry out for 1 hour.

For the chocolate cream, whisk the chilled mixture and sandwich them together with the chocolate cream. Place in paper cases.

Coffee macaroons

Prep and cook time: 1 hour ＊ makes: 40

INGREDIENTS:

4 egg whites
1 tsp lemon juice
250 g | 9 oz | 1 cup sugar
250 g | 9 oz | 1 cup ground almonds
2 tbsp strong espresso

To decorate:
30 ml | 1 fl. oz coffee liqueur
100 g | 3 ½ oz | ½ cup icing
(confectioners') sugar
50 chocolate covered coffee beans

METHOD:

Heat the oven to 140°C (120° fan) 275F, gas 1 and line 2 large baking trays with greaseproof paper.

Whisk the egg whites with the lemon juice until stiff. Gradually whisk in the sugar until thick and shiny.

Stir in the ground almonds and coffee powder.

Spoon small rounds on to a baking tray. Bake for 30-40 minutes until firm. Cool on the baking trays for a few minutes, then place on a wire rack to cool completely.

To decorate, put the coffee liqueur in a bowl and sift in the icing sugar. Stir until smooth.

Put into a small piping bag and pipe (or drizzle) on top of the macaroons. Place a coffee bean on top of each macaroon and leave them to set.

Nut macaroons

Prep and cook time: 45 minutes * makes: 40

INGREDIENTS:

4 egg whites
200 g | 7 oz | 1 cup light brown sugar
1 tsp lemon juice
150 g | 5 oz | 1 cup ground
hazelnuts (cobnuts)
100 g | 3 ½ oz | ¾ cup ground almonds

To decorate:
chocolate hazelnut spread
40 hazelnut halves

METHOD:

Heat the oven to 160°C (140° fan) 325F, gas 3.

Whisk the egg whites until they are very stiff. Gradually add the sugar and lemon juice, whisking all the time.

Fold in the ground nuts. Spoon small heaps of the mixture on to a baking tray and bake for 30-35 minutes until golden brown. Cool the macaroons on the baking tray for a few minutes, then place on a wire rack to cool completely.

Spoon the hazelnut spread on top of each macaroon and top with half a hazelnut.

Iced chocolate macaroons

Prep and cook time: 45 minutes ∗ makes: 20

INGREDIENTS:

125 g | 4 ½ oz | 1 ¼ cups icing (confectioners') sugar
1 tbsp cocoa powder
100 g | 3 ½ oz | ¾ cup ground almonds
2 egg whites

To decorate:
icing sugar

METHOD:

Heat the oven to 180°C (160° fan) 350F, gas 4 and line a large baking tray with greaseproof paper.

Sift the icing sugar and cocoa into a bowl, then stir in the ground almonds.

Whisk the egg whites until stiff and fold them into the dry ingredients until combined. Place small spoonfuls of the mixture onto the baking tray and leave to stand for 10 minutes to dry.

Bake for 15-20 minutes until firm. Cool on the baking tray for a few minutes, then place them on a wire rack to cool completely. To decorate, sift the icing sugar over the macaroons.

Aniseed macaroons

Prep and cook time: 1 hour 45 minutes * makes: 14

INGREDIENTS:

2 eggs
225 g | 8 oz | 2 ¼ cups icing
(confectioners') sugar
2 tsp grated lemon zest
2 tsp ground aniseed
250 g | 9 oz | 2 ¼ cups plain
(all-purpose) flour
½ tsp baking powder
1 tbsp crushed aniseed

METHOD:

Whisk the eggs and icing sugar until thick and light. Stir in the lemon zest and ground aniseed.

Sift in the flour and baking powder and mix well to form a dough. Wrap the dough in cling film and chill for 1 hour.

Roll out the dough on a lightly floured surface, to a 1 cm / ½ " thickness. Use a small, smooth-edged cutter to cut small rounds and place them on baking trays lined with greaseproof paper. Sprinkle with aniseed and leave to stand uncovered, overnight.

Heat the oven to 180°C (160° fan) 350F, gas 4.

Bake the macaroons for 25-30 minutes, until cooked and firm, but still pale. Cool on the baking tray for a few minutes, then place on a wire rack to cool completely.

Pistachio macaroons

Prep and cook time: 55 minutes * makes: 16

INGREDIENTS:

30 g | 1 oz | ⅓ cup unsalted pistachios,
finely chopped
125 g | 4 ½ oz | ¾ cup ground almonds
200 g | 7 oz | 2 cups icing
(confectioners') sugar
3 egg whites
green food dye

METHOD:

Mix the pistachios and almonds together. Whisk the egg
whites until stiff, then gradually sift in the icing sugar,
whisking all the time.

Add the almond mixture to the egg whites and gently
fold together. Add the green food dye.

Place spoonfuls of the mixture, evenly spaced, on a baking
tray lined with greaseproof paper. Set them aside for
30 minutes until a skin forms on top.

Heat the oven to 160°C (140° fan) 325F, gas 3.

Bake for about 15 minutes until firm. Cool the macaroons
on the baking tray for a few minutes, then place them on
a wire rack to cool completely.

Pecan macaroons

Prep and cook time: 30 minutes * makes: 15-20

INGREDIENTS:

250 g | 9 oz | 2 cups pecan
nuts, chopped
120 g | 4 oz | 1 ¼ cups icing sugar
2 large egg whites
a pinch of salt
2-3 drops vanilla extract
15-20 pecan halves

METHOD:

Heat the oven to 160°C (140° fan) 325F, gas 3 and line
a large baking tray with greaseproof paper.

Grind 200 g of the chopped pecans and the icing sugar
together in a food processor to a fine texture.

Whisk the egg whites with the salt until they are stiff.
Stir in the pecan mixture with the vanilla and the remaining
chopped pecans.

Place spoonfuls of the mixture on the baking tray and place
a pecan half on each macaroon.

Bake for 10-20 minutes, until very light brown. Cool on the
baking tray for a few minutes, then place on a wire rack to
cool completely.

Mocha macaroons

Prep and cook time: 30 minutes * makes: 30

INGREDIENTS:

4 egg whites
200 g | 7 oz | 2 cups icing
(confectioners') sugar
20 g | ¾ oz | ⅓ cup cornflour (cornstarch)
250 g | 9 oz | 1 ½ cups ground almonds
30 ml | 1 fl. oz instant coffee
75 g | 2 ½ oz | ¾ cup dark (plain)
chocolate, grated

For the filling and decoration:
60 g | 2 oz | ⅓ cup dark
chocolate, chopped
60 g | 2 oz | ¼ cup butter
1 egg yolk
80 g | 3 oz | ¾ cup icing
(confectioners') sugar
30 ml | 1 fl. oz instant coffee

METHOD:

Heat the oven to 160°C (140° fan) 325F, gas 3. Line a large
baking tray with greaseproof paper.

Whisk the egg whites until stiff, then whisk in the icing sugar
and cornflour until the mixture is stiff and shiny.

Fold in the almonds, coffee and chocolate until combined.

Spoon small rounds onto the baking tray. Bake for 15 minutes
until firm. Cool on the baking tray for a few minutes, then place
on a wire rack to cool completely.

For the filling, melt the chopped chocolate in a heatproof
bowl over a pan of simmering water.

Beat the butter until creamy, then beat in the egg yolk,
icing sugar and coffee. Stir in the chocolate until smooth.

Sandwich the macaroons with the cooled mocha filling
and drizzle the remaining chocolate cream over the top
of the macaroons.

Lübeck coconut macaroons

Prep and cook time: 35 minutes * makes: 30

INGREDIENTS:

1 egg white
a pinch of salt
50 g | 2 oz | ¼ cup sugar
½ lemon, juice
2 tsp grated lemon zest
100 g | 3 ½ oz marzipan, finely chopped
100 g | 3 ½ oz | 1 ⅓ cups desiccated (flaked)coconut

To decorate:
120 g | 4 oz dark (plain) chocolate

METHOD:

Heat the oven to 160°C (140° fan) 325F, gas 3. Line a large baking tray with greaseproof paper.

Whisk the egg white until stiff. Gradually add the salt, sugar, lemon juice and zest and continue whisking until very stiff.

Add the marzipan and coconut and stir until combined.

Put small teaspoonfuls apart on the baking tray and bake for 25 minutes.

To decorate, melt the chocolate in a heatproof bowl over a pan of simmering water. Dip the cooled macaroons halfway into the chocolate and leave to set.

Raspberry macaroons

Prep and cook time: 1 hour 25 minutes * makes: 10

INGREDIENTS:

125 g | 4 ½ oz | 1 cup ground almonds
200 g | 7 oz | 2 cups icing
(confectioners') sugar
3 egg whites
½ tsp cream of tartar
30 g | 1 oz caster (superfine) sugar
2 tsp raspberry extract
30 g | 1 oz raspberries, pureed

METHOD:

Mix the ground almonds and icing sugar together. Set aside.

Whisk the egg whites in a mixing bowl until stiff peaks form. Slowly whisk in the cream of tartar, caster sugar, raspberry puree and raspberry extract until the mixture is smooth and glossy.

Gently fold in the ground almonds and icing sugar.

Spoon 5 cm / 2 " rounds onto a baking tray lined with greaseproof paper. Leave them to stand for 1 hour until no longer sticky to the touch.

Heat the oven to 160°C (140° fan) 325F, gas 3.

Bake for 10-15 minutes, until cooked through. Leave to cool for 5 minutes. Carefully peel away the baking paper and set aside to cool completely.

Chocolate chestnut macaroons

Prep and cook time: 2 hours * makes: 20

INGREDIENTS:

125 g | 4 ½ oz | 1 cup ground almonds
250 g | 9 oz | 2 ½ cups icing
(confectioners') sugar
3 egg whites
30 g | 1 oz | ¼ cup caster
(superfine) sugar

For the filling:
50 g | 2 oz | ⅓ cup chopped
dark (plain) chocolate
200 ml | 7 fl. oz | ⅞ cup cream
45 g | 1 ½ oz chestnut butter

METHOD:

Stir the ground almonds and icing sugar together. Whisk the egg whites until they form stiff peaks. Add the caster sugar and whisk until the mixture is stiff and glossy.

Gently fold the mixture into the ground almonds and icing sugar until smooth.

Spoon, or pipe, 40 small rounds, evenly spaced, onto baking trays lined with greaseproof paper. Leave the trays to stand for 15 minutes to allow a skin to form on the macaroons.

Heat the oven to 190°C (170° fan) 375F, gas 5.

Bake for 10-15 minutes until firm. Cool the macaroons on the baking trays for a few minutes, then place on a wire rack to cool completely.

For the filling, melt the chocolate in a heatproof bowl over a pan of simmering water, then set it aside to cool slightly.

Whisk the cream until it is thick. Stir in the chestnut butter and melted chocolate. Chill for an hour until firm. Sandwich the macaroons in pairs with the chestnut cream.

Classic macaroons

Prep and cook time: 40 minutes ∗ makes: 20-30

INGREDIENTS:

175 g | 6 oz | 1 ¾ cups icing
(confectioners') sugar
125 g | 4 ½ oz | ¾ cup ground almonds
3 large egg whites
75 g | 2 ½ oz | ⅓ cup caster
(superfine) sugar
a pinch of salt
pink, green, yellow and brown food dye

METHOD:

Blend the icing sugar and ground almonds in a food processor
until very fine.

Whisk the egg whites with the salt until soft peaks form.
Gradually whisk in the caster sugar until the mixture is thick
and glossy.

Fold the almond and icing sugar mixture into the meringue
and mix well.

Divide the mixture into separate bowls and add a few drops
of food dye to each bowl.

Spoon or pipe the mixture in small rounds onto 2 baking
trays lined with greaseproof paper. Leave the macaroons
to stand for 10-15 minutes to form a slight skin.

Heat the oven to 160°C (140° fan) 325F gas 3.

Bake for 15 minutes until firm. While the macaroons are
still warm, sandwich the rounds together in pairs and then
allow them to cool completely on a wire rack.

Almond macaroons

Prep and cook time: 1 hour 20 minutes * makes: 16

INGREDIENTS:

100 g | 3 ½ oz dark (plain) chocolate
3 egg whites
150 g | 5 oz | 1 cup ground almonds
150 g | 5 oz | ¾ cup caster
(superfine) sugar
1 tbsp cocoa powder

For the filling:
100 ml | 3 ½ fl. oz cream
100 g | 3 ½ oz plain chocolate
1 tbsp unsalted butter

METHOD:

Heat the oven to 140°C (120° fan) 275F, gas 1.

Line a large baking tray with greaseproof paper. Melt the chocolate in a small pan set over a bowl of gently simmering water. Whisk the egg whites until they form soft peaks and set aside.

Mix the almonds, sugar and cocoa powder together and gently fold into the egg whisked egg whites. Add the melted chocolate and mix gently until smooth.

Drop 32 small spoonfuls of the mixture onto the baking tray and gently flatten the tops. Bake for 1 hour. Cool on the baking trays for a few minutes, then place the macaroons on a wire rack to cool completely.

For the filling, heat the cream to boiling point. Put the chocolate in a small bowl then pour over the hot cream. Mix gently, then stir in the butter and allow it to cool. Beat well with a wooden spoon until the filling is thick and fluffy, then sandwich the macaroons together.

Tea time macaroons

Prep and cook time: 40 minutes * makes: 20

INGREDIENTS:

175 g | 6 oz | 1 ¼ cups icing
(confectioners') sugar
125 g | 4 ½ oz | 1 cup ground almonds
3 large egg whites
75 g | 2 ½ oz | ⅓ cup caster
(superfine) sugar
1 tsp raspberry extract
pink food dye
1 tbsp unsalted pistachios,
finely chopped
green food dye

For the filling:
200 ml | 7 fl. oz | ⅞ cup cream
1 tbsp icing sugar
few drops vanilla extract

METHOD:

Grind the icing sugar and ground almonds in a food processor
until the mixture is very fine.

Whisk the egg whites to soft peaks, then gradually whisk in
the caster sugar until thick and glossy. Fold in the almond
and icing sugar mixture until it is smooth.

Divide the mixture into 2 bowls. Add the raspberry extract
and pink dye to a bowl and the pistachios and green dye to
the other bowl.

Spoon or pipe 40 small rounds onto a baking tray lined with
greaseproof paper. Leave the trays to stand for 10-15 minutes.

Heat the oven to 160°C (140° fan) 325F, gas 3. Bake the
macaroons for 15 minutes until firm. Cool on the baking trays
for a few minutes, then place on a wire rack to cool completely.

For the filling, whisk the cream, icing sugar and vanilla until stiff.
Sandwich the cooled macaroons with the cream filling.

INDEX.

INDEX.

INDEX.